WITHSTANDING

THE WINDS

WITHSTANDING
AN ENCOURAGING DEVOTIONAL JOURNAL
THE WINDS
CHARMAIN GRIFFITHS

Tate Publishing & Enterprises

Withstanding the Winds
Copyright © 2011 by Charmain Griffiths. All rights reserved.

No part of this publication may be reproduced, stored in a retrieval system or transmitted in any way by any means, electronic, mechanical, photocopy, recording or otherwise without the prior permission of the author except as provided by USA copyright law.

Scripture quotations marked "NIV" are taken from the *Holy Bible, New International Version* ®, Copyright © 1973, 1978, 1984 by International Bible Society. Used by permission of Zondervan Publishing House. All rights reserved.

Scripture quotations marked "MSG" are taken from *The Message*, Copyright © 1993, 1994, 1995, 1996, 2000, 2001, 2002. Used by permission of NavPress Publishing Group. All rights reserved.

Scripture quotations marked "CEV" are from the *Holy Bible; Contemporary English Version,* Copyright © 1995, Barclay M. Newman, ed., American Bible Society. Used by permission. All rights reserved.

Scripture quotations marked (ASV) are taken from the *American Standard Version,* Copyright © 1901, Thomas Nelson & Sons. Used by permission. All rights reserved.

Scripture quotations marked (KJV) are taken from the *Holy Bible, King James Version*, Copyright © 1769, Cambridge,. Used by permission. All rights reserved.

Scripture quotations marked (NKJV) are taken from the *New King James Version*, Copyright © 1982 by Thomas Nelson, Inc. Used by permission. All rights reserved.

The opinions expressed by the author are not necessarily those of Tate Publishing, LLC.

Published by Tate Publishing & Enterprises, LLC
127 E. Trade Center Terrace | Mustang, Oklahoma 73064 USA
1.888.361.9473 | www.tatepublishing.com

Tate Publishing is committed to excellence in the publishing industry. The company reflects the philosophy established by the founders, based on Psalm 68:11,
"The LORD gave the word and great was the company of those who published it."

Book design copyright © 2011 by Tate Publishing, LLC. All rights reserved.
Cover design by Kristen Verser
Interior design by Sarah Kirchen

Published in the United States of America
ISBN: 978-1-61739-987-9
Religion / Christian Life / Inspirational
11.02.10

"So speak encouraging words to one another. Build up hope so you'll all be together in this, no one left out, no one left behind. I know you're already doing this; just keep on doing it."

1 Thessalonians 5:11 (MSG)

TABLE OF CONTENTS

SECTION I
Fear & Unrest 11

SECTION II
Worry & Anxiety 53

SECTION III
Frustration & Disappointment 93

SECTION IV
Despair & Defeat 143

SECTION V
Doubt & Insecurity 195

Wind:

a tendency or force that influences events

SECTION I
FEAR & UNREST

There is a song I love to sing in part that goes, "I know the Peace Speaker, and I know Him by name." In times of difficulty and confusion, I sing it, and it helps to calm my fears and bring me to a place of surety—a place where I can feel "solidness" under my feet even though I may be sailing through the rough waters of life.

The song reminds me of an account recorded by the Apostle Mark's Gospel, chapter 4:35–41, about Jesus and His disciples sailing across the sea in a boat when a windstorm arose. Mark tells us that Jesus was asleep at the time when the winds were raging, and the disciples were struggling to keep the boat safe in the turbulent waters. Someone woke Jesus up and pretty much asked Him (paraphrased): "What's up with that? What kind of behavior is this you are showing, sleeping while we are fighting to stay alive?"

Can you just picture the scene? Jesus is asleep on a pillow, his demeanor restful, and his clothes still dry and in order while his disciples (his followers) are all exhausted, in disarray, stricken with fear, wet clothes clinging to them. Whew! Then Jesus does the unimaginable thing:

"And he arose, and rebuked the wind, and said unto the sea, Peace, be still. And the wind ceased, and there was a great calm" (Mark 4:39–40 KJV).

He spoke to his followers: "Why are you so fearful? How is it that you have no faith?"

Jesus is still speaking these same words. I don't know about you, but I find that in my moment of greatest need,

Jesus always *seems* not to be there. Like He is asleep while I am getting frustrated, discouraged, and tired. It is at this my weakest point, when all my energy is depleted, that I remember: I know the peace speaker. I know Him by name. What a relief!

Word of Encouragement:
There is no need to be fearful about the storms of life. They will blow over. They will try to scare and shake you up. To be honest, sometimes for a moment it will seem like they have succeeded. As if any minute now everything will be lost. Take your eyes off the storm and go below (on your knees) and find Jesus. He is on board; and yes, He is *not* perturbed by the present situation. He is in control.

Be blessed always.

_____
_____
_____
_____

My prayer today:

_____
_____
_____
_____

"My beloved spake, and said unto me, Rise up, my love, my fair one, and come away. For, lo, the winter is past, the rain is over and gone."
                    Songs of Solomon 2:10–11 (KJV)

Stop the running…there is no place left for you to go

*You have danced to the beat of
negative thinking long enough*

*You have drank the wine of guilt
until you now have a stench*

*That you cannot wash away with
offerings and sacrifices*

You have been in this place a long time

Why are you so despondent, my child?

Have I not cared for you?

*Did I not answer when you cried and
you thought your life was over?*

*Did I not open doors for you and
gave you new beginnings?*

Yet you worry about your tomorrow

You have no hope for your future

You are constantly complaining about your yesterdays

Today I want you to listen

To concentrate on what I am saying

Take your focus from the pressure that is building

And give me your undivided attention

Today let us reason together

I hold you as a Father who loves His children

And into your life I pour My Peace

My child, come closer to Me

And let the warmth of My Love embrace you

Rest your weary head upon My Shoulder

And lay your burden at My Feet

Take off the raiment of heaviness

And put on the garment of praise

Wash your hands and face with the lather of My Words

Eat from my banquet table

For I will never leave you nor forsake you

I will always protect you

My child...it is time to stop running

You have been in this state long enough

Be blessed always.

_____
_____
_____
_____

My prayer today:

_____
_____
_____
_____

∞

> For he shall give his angels charge over thee, to keep thee in all thy ways. They shall bear thee up in their hands, lest thou dash thy foot against a stone.
> Psalm 91:11–12 (KJV)

A podiatrist held a seminar at my church recently and told us many people break their toes during the nighttime when they wake up to make night trips and, without any form of lighting, would hit their foot against the furniture, even the well-known surroundings of their own bedroom. I winced when she said it, because the scene was all too familiar for me. I'd wake up, *barely,* and try to make my way to the bathroom without totally losing my sleep. I would be doing fine and then *bam!* I'd hit my pinkie toe against something that has always been there, and the pain takes away any sleep that was left in me.

It is in your night season when your vision is blurred by circumstances that the little accidents of life come to stop your process in God. Here you are doing great. Got your testimony, got your shout on, walked away from that temptation, kept your mouth shut when you could have otherwise, and you are finally moving into what seems like a place of security and destiny. Then it happens. You have one moment when your guard was down, one moment when you relaxed, one moment of weakness. Thank God He does not wait for us to have a problem before He sends us a solution.

Angels. I have always loved learning about angels. I am somewhat fascinated by them and always read with envy any account of people who have had angelic visitation. Angels are ministering beings that God uses in various capacities. I was taught as a child that I had my own angel assigned to me. Well, I am not sure if this is true, but I do know that throughout scriptures God had sent angels to minister to mankind in the time of need.

Word of Encouragement:
God got you in His hands, and His eyes are watching over you. He calls you the apple of His eye and promises that "no evil shall befall you" (Psalm 91:10 KJV). God has angels on the lookout, watching for your well-being. He wants

you to be watchful, never letting your guard down. It's your night season, and your fear may be trying to stop you from reaching your place of destiny. But keep on moving, knowing that you are protected under the mighty hand of God.

Be blessed always.

_____
_____
_____
_____
_____

My prayer today:

_____
_____
_____
_____
_____

God is Love.
Love is such a powerful word. It is the wonder of heaven that God would love us while we were yet sinners. Yes, God loved us first. It was not that we acknowledged Him and He in turn bestowed His love on us. No, we disobeyed

Him, rebelled against Him, and while He had the power and the right to destroy us, He instead loved us. *Whew!*

For most of us, expressing love to a loving God is relatively easy. God is perfect and His love is unconditional. To love our brother, however, can be challenging, especially if he or she is a "sandpaper" person—you know, a person who rubs you the wrong way. Oh, how I wish we could chose our brothers; like buying fruit at the store I would pick the best-looking ones, but it is just not like that. God gives us a variety of people to associate with and each helps us in some way, even the "sandpaper" people. We have to love them all. We probably think we have valid reasons why someone doesn't deserve our love. Love them anyway. John states:

> If a man says, I love God, and hateth his brother, he is a liar: for he that loveth not his brother whom he hath seen, how can he love God whom he hath not seen? And this commandment have we from him, That he who loveth God love his brother also.
>
> 1 John 4:20–21 (KJV)

Word of Encouragement:
Find ways to express your love to your brother, family, friends, coworkers, neighbors, and church family. Maybe all you can do is pray for them or just give a smile, but ask God to let His love shine through you to others. The world can be an ugly place. Let's beautify it with the Love of God.

God is Love.

Be blessed always.

_____
_____
_____
_____

My prayer today:

_____
_____
_____
_____

※

Unless you've been living under a rock, you know that there is a shaking going on all around us—the economy, politics, religion, morality, you name it; and we have seen a shaking from the core of its existence. Scripture tells us that David had experience with troublesome times as he pens in Psalm 46:1–3 (KJV) that

> God is our refuge and strength, a very present help in trouble. Therefore will not we fear, though the earth be removed, and though the mountains be carried into the midst of the sea; Though the waters thereof

roar and be troubled, though the mountains shake with the swelling thereof. Selah

It is evident that there is going to be a shifting in our lives. I don't believe this is an advertising hoax or just a political maneuver. We have embarked on some tough times where even the affluent amongst us are becoming somewhat frugal. If our hope is in the government, church, job, education, or people, we are going to be in trouble. Don't believe that the "earth" you have so firmly placed your feet upon cannot be moved. And don't think that the "mountain" you are using for safety cannot be replaced.

We have one sure fountain that will withstand the elements of time—Jesus Christ. The songwriter must have had a glimpse of this situation when he penned the words "On Christ the solid rock I stand; all other ground is sinking sand."

So what are we going to do in these trying times? I declare that I will not fear. I refuse to be paralyzed into doing nothing by the spirit of fear. *God is...therefore, I am.* I am more than what you see. I am able to do more than I can even imagine. Fear will immobilize us, but faith will give us wings to do the impossible. I pray we will all walk now in faith—that we will rebuke every negative spirit from around us and step out by faith into the unfamiliar. Who knows? When all this is over we can be better than when it all began.

Word of Encouragement:
Do not fear. My friends tell me I am a brave person and so this statement is easy for me to say. They could not be

further from the truth. Bravery has nothing to do with this. I learned a long time ago that nothing in this life is a guarantee. I have a few scars on my heart that can testify to this fact. I have been broken in enough places to understand that the only truth I have in this life is Jesus Christ. I believe, therefore I trust. Today let us hope in Him together. Sure the shaking is all around us and many of the things we thought would always be there will be removed; but God is. Selah—Amen—So let it be.

Be blessed always.

My prayer today:

Have you ever believed a lie? It is just awful because even after you have discovered the truth, the residue of the lie will still linger. Take, for example, if you were adopted and never told. You have lived you whole life thinking someone else is your mother/father and then...You get sick, and the doctors need to know you family history, and there you are, realizing you have based your whole life on a lie. Lies destroy lives. It's plain and simple—intentionally or not. "Deliver me from the liars, God! They smile so sweetly but lie through their teeth" (Psalm 120:2 MSG).

The LORD spoke to me in the silence of the night about not totally believing His words. It was one of those moments when my words were not matching what His words said, and the conflict was in my heart. The LORD told me then that if my thoughts and actions were not in line with His words then I had believed and was living a lie. It's plain and simple. He said when I look in the mirror if I do not believe what His words said about me being "fearfully and wonderfully made," then I have believed a lie. A half-truth is just a sugarcoated lie. It is a lie nonetheless. *Whew!* Think about it.

It is the trickery of the enemy to bring lies to our lives. The scriptures refer to Satan as "the father of lies" (John 8:44 KJV). Often lies are brought through our own family members and close friends. A father's careless words in a moment of anger can inject a lie in our lives. A disgruntled mother in a web of bitterness can fill our ears with lies. An overzealous friend in a need to shield us can bring lies into our lives. The question I have for you today is: Whose report will you believe?

Word of Encouragement:
It is high time to believe what God says. Living a life of mediocrity, feeling rejected and defeated, beaten down, and forgotten is a lie. God has called you to an abundant life. He has given you the Holy Spirit to lead and guide you. He has placed His anointing in you to equip you for a great and mighty work. Know who you are and live according to His words.

Be blessed always.

My prayer today:

It's time for action.
There are talks everywhere about the world being in a recession. Now, I am not an economist, so I don't qualify to speak on the topic, but *I do know* that the amount of money I am spending *out* for goods and services have increased, while the amount I am taking *in* has remained the same. Gas prices are up, grocery bills are up, homes are in foreclosures, jobs are being cut from large companies, and overall most people are in a state of uncertainty.

This situation reminds me of a time in the scripture when the children of Israel was under siege by the Syrians, and because of fear of the enemy no one was leaving the city. The people were starving, and there is even a record of cannibalism. While everyone just sat there immobilized, the Bible tells us about four lepers at the gate who decided to do something. They said to each other,

> Why sit we here until we die? If we say, we will enter into the city, then the famine is in the city, and we shall die there: and if we sit still here, we die also. Now therefore come, and let us fall unto the host of the Syrians: if they save us alive, we shall live; and if they kill us, we shall but die.
>
> 2 Kings 7:3–4 (KJV)

It's time for action. As children of God we are not helpless. I heard a preacher declare the other day, "We are not waiting on God; God is waiting on us." Whew! That was an eye opener! God wants us to live by faith and not by sight. Faith is not subject to the state of the economy. Faith is embedded in our trust and belief in God. Rethink your options. Maybe you have been stuck into one way of thinking, and God wants to give you a new freedom. A new career may emerge. You may even return to school and further educate yourself. Maybe you need to sublet your house to help with the payments and in turn God can use you to be a witness to someone. Maybe you have running from the call of God on your life, and as you lose things you will find that you are actually gaining it all. You can survive on less than you think.

Word of Encouragement:
Ask yourself this question: *Why sit here until you die when God is offering abundant life?* Remember the lepers in the story? Well, as they made their way to the Syrian camp, God miraculously moved on their behalf, and when they got there, the camps were empty and there was food everywhere. Don't give up, because your story has not yet ended. *It's time for action.*

Be blessed always.

_____
_____
_____
_____
_____

My prayer today:

_____
_____
_____
_____

His life was destined for failure, or so he thought. He was born blind and had always been a beggar. He knew what it felt like to live at the mercy of others dealing with their scorn and abuse. He's always been attentive to what was going on around him for his survival, and as he heard the crowd approach, he inquired what the noise was all about. It was Jesus of Nazareth passing by. *Hope against Hope.* . He started to cry out for Jesus to help him. After all, he had heard about this Jesus of Nazareth, the healer, Jehovah Rophe. The people around him got upset at his loud calling. They told him to shut up, but need along with desperation made him cry all the more. "Jesus stopped and said, 'Call him.' So they called to the blind man, 'Cheer up! On your feet! He's calling you'" (Mark 10:49, NIV). That day, he received his sight.

This story of Blind Bartimaaeus is about one man seizing the moment. Read the account in the Gospel of Mark, chapter 10. Understanding that the One who can *change* our situation is within our reach ought to make us press our way to Him. Unfortunately, we have so many resources at our disposal, we are so accepting with our shortcomings, and we get discouraged so easily that there is no real hunger or need pushing us to a point of desperation for God. I believe that God sends us many "moments" that we do not grab a hold of, "moments" that could change our lives. He invites us to have a relationship with him, yet we settle for mere religion. He orchestrates people into our life, yet we discount them as insignificant. He opens doors of opportunity for us to partner with Him, yet we walk right by without ever stepping in. Often it is only when trouble has come into our lives that we realize how many moments we have missed.

Word of Encouragement:
Jesus is passing by. Seize the moment. Do not be concerned about what the crowd around you is saying. Seize the moment. It is not God's will for you to live with anything that hinders your future, even if it is generational. Seize the moment. Today is the day, now is the time to walk into your blessing. Seize this moment and listen to the voice of the LORD calling you.

Be blessed always.

My prayer today:

_____
_____
_____
_____

Repentance. Now that's an unpopular word. According to Webster's dictionary it means "to be sorry; to recognize the wrong in something you have done and be sorry about it; to change one's ways." For some, the act of repenting is easy, especially when the wrong is primarily done to God, who is a perfect Being. It gets harder when it is our brother that we have wronged, seeing that they are as imperfect as we are.

The Bible gives an account of twin brothers Esau and Jacob in the book of Genesis. After a grand act of bribery and trickery, Jacob stole Esau's birthright and his blessings. As expected, Esau acted in response and threatened to kill his brother. As expected, Jacob ran away from home to save his life. Years later Jacob is ready to come home, but as he nears his destination, he knows he has to deal with the feud with Esau. He is expecting the worse, but the account gives us an element of surprise; as Jacob repents, Esau forgives him and embraces him. Read the account in Genesis 32–33.

Have you wronged anyone? Is the LORD speaking to you about an unresolved issue in your heart? Are you living in fear because of this? I find that when I delay repenting, my heart becomes like stone, and I am not broken. I find that the difficulty in repenting begins with me first admitting that I have done wrong. (Talk about looking at the face in the mirror.) David says, "The LORD is nigh unto them that are of a broken heart; and saveth such as be of a contrite spirit" (Psalm 34:18 KJV).

Word of Encouragement:
God loves you and wants you to walk in total peace and freedom. He knows that if seeds of pride germinate in your heart it will weigh you down and open the door for the enemy to produce within you feelings of guilt and despair. You will be pleasantly surprised at how much better you will feel after you repent.

Be blessed always.

_____
_____
_____
_____

My prayer today:

_____

_____

_____

_____

Have you ever asked yourself the question: can God really be trusted? Let's be honest. When you take a look at natural disasters, poverty and hunger, crime inflicted upon innocent children, the inequalities in life, bad things happening to good people, you may for a moment wonder if God can be trusted with your life and your heart.

Things aren't always what they seem. That's a lesson life has taught me. I have to concede that I do not know it all, and frankly, I don't have all the answers to all the questions life asks. When I am asked the tough questions, I do not worry about exposing my limitedness; after all, I am human. But God is infinite. God is a Spirit. He does not operate on the same level as I do. He is omniscient.

> For my thoughts are not your thoughts, neither are your ways my ways, saith the Lord. For as the heavens are higher than the earth, so are my ways higher than your ways, and my thoughts than your thoughts.
>
> Isaiah 55: 8–9 (KJV)

I thought about the Apostle Peter's experience of walking on water as recorded in Matthew chapter fourteen. "Peter said to Him, "Lord, if it is You, command me to come to You on the water." And He said, "Come!" And Peter got out of the boat, and walked on the water and came toward Jesus" (Matthew 14:28–29 NAS). Can you imagine how Peter must have felt when Jesus said to him, "Come"? In that one moment he had to make a decision. Can I really trust Jesus? Look at what is happening all around. The winds are howling and the waters are unstable. Peter made a choice to trust the King of glory. And that choice allowed him to defy the laws of nature, and he got a miracle in his life.

Word of Encouragement:
Trust God always. Sure, you will have questions and ask them if you must but at the end of the day, know that God can be trusted. He promised you that His word would not return to Him void before it accomplishes everything He has sent it to do. In other words, if God said it, then that settles it. One word from the Lord can change you eternally. "For I know the thoughts that I think toward you, saith the Lord, thoughts of peace, and not of evil, to give you an expected end" (Jeremiah 29:11 KJV).

Be blessed always.

_____
_____
_____
_____
_____

My prayer today:

_____
_____
_____
_____
_____

It is said if life throws you lemons then you should go ahead and make lemonade. Hilarious isn't it? There is always a brighter side to life no matter how dark it gets. But lemonade needs more than lemons to make it happen. It needs water and, oh yes, a sweetener.

My mind reflects on the story of Lazarus, the brother of Mary and Martha, as recorded in John 11. Jesus was a friend of the family, so when Lazarus got sick the sisters sent for Jesus to heal him. Jesus did not respond immediately, as expected, and Lazarus eventually died. After the fourth day, Jesus showed up amidst a household of mourners. He asked to be taken to the graveside of Lazarus and assured Martha that "thy brother shall rise again" (John 11:23 KJV). We know from Scripture that Lazarus did rise that day, and Jesus did fulfill his word.

I can testify that life at times has tossed me a ball (lemon), a circumstance that is brutal at best. It may be sickness for some, a financial situation for others, or a relationship issue that is having an impact on not just you but others around you. You may have cried until you have enough tears (water). Hold it. Don't give in; don't give up. You will have lemonade before all this is over. Why? Because you have the promise (sweetener) of God's word. "For all the promises of God in him are yea, and in him Amen, unto the glory of God by us" (2 Corinthians 1:20 KJV). Isn't it refreshing to know that Jesus will stand by His every word to you?

Word of Encouragement:
Do not be intimidated by the circumstances of life. You have an advocate, a high priest who can sympathize with your weaknesses. You have all ingredients for a miracle, and yes, your change is on the way.

Be blessed always.

_____
_____
_____
_____

My prayer today:

_____
_____
_____
_____

> Behold, how good and how pleasant it is for brethren to dwell together in unity!
>
> Psalm 133:1 (KJV)

Unity is a lifetime pursuit, even when it involves a circle of the folks we love and respect, because essentially people are as different as their faces are. When we extend that circle to include coworkers, neighbors, and church members, the situation is even more complicated because we can choose to disassociate ourselves from people we don't get along with. Add to that cultural differences, race, and gender, and getting any sort of agreement amongst us is almost impossible.

In my own life I have struggled with the issue of unity. No, I am not an unbearable person, nor do I stir up strife amongst others; I consider myself private. This means I absolutely, positively do not allow anyone into my space without an invitation. It may sound aloof, but, in essence, it just means that I have an underlying self-esteem issue that I am dealing with. Now you know! The good news is, God is really working with me to deal with it. When I relocated to Georgia, God gave me the desire to have fellowship with people outside my culture.

Now this was challenging, because my whole life has always been with my "own people." He has placed me in a church where the culture was diverse, the congregation was mixed, and the leadership style was opposite to what I was accustomed to. At first I was lost because this was so much unlike me, but gradually, as I yielded to God's will, He brought unity into my life and worship. *Hallelujah!*

Word of Encouragement:
Disunity is not God's plan for your life. He wants you to have genuine fellowship with one another because in unity there is strength. There is so much to gain in having unity, because "one can chase a thousand, but two can put ten thousand to flight" (Deuteronomy 32:30 KJV). Reach out today to someone; it is pleasant, and it is good.

Be blessed always.

My prayer today:

_____
_____
_____
_____

※

> Be of good courage, and He shall strengthen your heart, all ye that hope in the Lord.
>
> Psalm 31:24 (NKJV)

Embarking on a new venture can be challenging. Moving to a new city, starting a new job, or returning to school. Even in our relationship with God, when it shifts to a new level, the unfamiliarity of it can be unsettling. Of course we want changes, we even pray for them, but when they come we can still be apprehensive about them. Are we doing the right thing? Can we really handle this? Is this God's will? Is this too ambitious of a move? These are some of the questions that flow through our minds as we contemplate a transition.

I have had some recent transitions in my life that have left me feeling like I was on a roller-coaster ride. Normally, when I go to a theme park, I am not one to get on those rides—at least not now. In my younger days, I used to wait in lines just to get the thrill of the rides. Now I am more cautious and selective. I wonder if my need to be so careful has hindered me in experiencing new things in God. As I grow older, I want more security of the "sameness" of every day. I find that God, on the other hand, wants to take me to new heights in Him. He wants me to trust Him more and to let go completely. He wants the security I have to be in Him.

We see this behavior in our children. When they are a one-year-old, we can say to them "jump," and they will let go—careless abandon—and be in our arms, but when they get to three years old, they may trust, but you can tell they are now calculating the risk factor involved. "Trust in the LORD with all thine heart; and lean not unto thine own understanding" (Proverbs 3:5 KJV).

Word of Encouragement:
Let go and let God. If God brings you to a door, walk through it. Keep on moving. It will get easier with each step. Build up your courage and just do it. He promises that He will be with your always.

Be blessed always.

_____
_____
_____
_____
_____

My prayer today:

_____
_____
_____
_____

※

My garage door has not worked properly for the last couple of weeks. I am not sure how it happened, but the remote will not lift it all the way. Someone has to manually help open it each time we drive out. My husband has tried fixing it several times and, after *all* failed attempts, has conceded that we need to call an expert. But we have not called one yet. Why? Because we have slowly gotten used to the deficiency. Even though it is an inconvenience, we had adjusted our comings and goings to the shortcoming.

I am reminded of a story I heard about a frog. It goes that if you place a frog in a pot of boiling water and leave it uncovered, the frog will immediately leap out of the pot or at least try to. However, if you place this same frog in a pot of cold water, leave it uncovered, and place heat under the pot, the frog will adjust its body to the changing heat and will eventually boil to death. The frog will never make an attempt to leap out. Frightening, isn't it? "There's a way of life that looks harmless enough; look again—it leads straight to hell. Sure, those people appear to be having a good time, but all that laughter will end in heartbreak" (Proverbs 14:12–13 MSG).

The enemy's trickery can be so subtle that, like the frog, we keep adjusting and adjusting until our consciences become dead to the things of God. How many times have we settled for less than what God has in store for us? How much sin does it really take to corrupt a person? How much tolerance should one have before going over the edge? How close to the other side do we want to be without going over? How many more "lukewarm" services will our churches hold before we shout enough is enough? "The stupid ridicule right and wrong, but a moral life is a favored life" (Proverbs 14:9 MSG).

Word of Encouragement:
God wants you to be all he has created you to be. Every now and again, check your life and make sure that you are living to your full potential. Maybe you need to call in the "expert" Jesus Christ to fix the broken issues of your lives. He specializes in the things that seem impossible. It is not God's will for you to sit like the frog and adjust to the environment around you. Be proactive. Take the high road and walk in the integrity of God's Word.

Be blessed always.

_____
_____
_____
_____

My prayer today:

_____
_____
_____
_____

∽⚭∽

I laid me down and slept; I awaked; for the Lord sustained me.

Psalm 3:5 (kjv)

The storms of economic turmoil have been raging for a while now. We have seen the uprooting of business giants collapsing under the pressure from the winds of insecurity. You don't have to be without a job or in the throngs of foreclosure to understand that times are tough, and people are struggling daily to provide the basics—food, shelter, and clothing. Know this, storms—*financial, relational, spiritual,* or whatever you are facing—are a part of life.

Some storms are created by our own negligence, impatience, mistakes, misunderstanding, lust, greed, pride, selfishness—in other words, by our own doing. Others may be a result of an attack from the enemy or just an end product of the sinful state of mankind. But whatever the origin, storms are meant to drown us in misery, uproot our faith, and cause us to give up and walk away from the destiny that God has planned for us. *God forbid!*

We can be reassured that God knows the storms that are brewing in our lives. He knows just where we are. The scriptures tell us that David was no stranger to storms. Even before he was anointed to be king of Israel, David weathered the storms in the form of a lion and a bear in the hillside as he tended his father's sheep. He had to face the giant Goliath and then run for his life as King Saul pursued, wanting to kill him. Yes, David was familiar with storms! He even had to deal with a coup attempt from his son Absalom.

Read 2 Samuel 15. Can you imagine being attack by those closest to you? Those whom should love you are now behaving like your enemies. And the hand that you are using to feed someone suddenly becomes bitten. *Ouch! Be watchful in this hour!* It was during this particular storm that David penned Psalm 3.

A storm can drain you of everything—spiritually, emotionally, mentally, financially—you name it. I remember my first "natural" storm and the howling sounds the wind made. It was like the echoes of the soundtrack of a horror movie intensified. I know from experience that sleep is hard to come by during a storm. But God wants you to trust him.

Word of Encouragement:
If you do nothing else for the remainder of this year, do this one thing: stake all your hopes and confidence in the God who loves and cares for you; the only One who has proven He can withstand any storm. David tells us that God is "the lifter up of mine head" (Psalm 3:3 KJV). I encourage you to rest in the midst of your storm. Confuse the enemy. Refuse to live in fear and trust God to sustain you in it all.

Be blessed always.

_____
_____
_____
_____
_____

My prayer today:

_____
_____
_____
_____
_____

> Instead you thrill to God's Word; you chew on Scripture day and night. You're a tree replanted in Eden, bearing fresh fruit every month. Never dropping a leaf, always in blossom"
>
> (Psalm 1:2–3 MSG).

My days are getting busier and busier. With work, school, children, housework, spouse, church, and me, I can hardly find time to sleep. Not good at all. Of course the right answer would be to balance them all or take an item off the list, but unfortunately these are all important aspects of my life, and any adjustment in one would have an effect on the other. To top this off, I am expected to be a full-time student of the Word of God. I *should* be able to say that I spend at least one hour each day just studying the Word, but I must confess this is often not true. Some days I can hardly get five minutes of reading in, if any at all, and by the end of the week I feel spiritually drained, sluggish, short tempered, and out of sync. Have you ever been there?

David advised us in Psalm 119:11 how he got balance into his life. "Thy word have I hid in mine heart, that I might not sin against thee." The digesting of the Word operates pretty much the same way food works for our natural bodies. When we eat healthy meals, our body takes the nutrients and "hides" it within our cells and releases it as needed. If we eat junk food—that cannot be hidden because the body does not need it—it is stored as fat. Fat makes us sluggish, short tempered—you get the picture. Eating right is part of maintaining a healthy lifestyle.

Word of Encouragement:
Daily dosage of the Word of God should not be optional. If your attitude is out of "whack" and fear seems to be your constant friend, it is time to get rid of the junk that you're allowing your spirit to absorb. Get your Bible and sit down for some quiet time with the LORD. It will change your life.

Be blessed always.

_____
_____
_____
_____
_____

My prayer today:

_____
_____
_____
_____
_____

Years ago I heard the story about the man who lost everything and was so despondent that he decided to commit suicide by hanging. He made a knot with a rope and then had his last meal—one banana. He tossed the banana peel and was making his way to the rope, when he caught a sight that stopped him in his steps. He saw another man walk by, pick up the banana peel he had just tossed, and start eating it. *His perspective changed immediately.* In the end, he decided to keep on living. The main point of the story: no matter how bad you think your situation is chances are someone is going through something similar or worse than you.

The scriptures give an account of an experience that the Prophet Elisha and his servant had that teaches us how important it is to have the proper perspective. It was during the earlier years of Elisha's ministry when the king of Syria warred against the king of Israel and it was because of Elisha prophetic insight that he was able to help save Israel. The Syrian king was furious when he learned about Elisha's help, and, in retaliation, he sent his armies to destroy him.

> And when the servant of the man of God was risen early, and gone forth, behold, an host compassed the city both with horses and chariots. And his servant said unto him, Alas, my master! how shall we do? And he answered, *Fear not: for they that be with us are more than they that be with them.* And

Elisha prayed, and said, L ORD, I pray thee, *open his eyes, that he may see.* And the L ORD opened the eyes of the young man; and he saw: and, behold, the mountain was full of horses and chariots of fire round about Elisha.

2 Kings 6:15–17 (KJV)

Word of Encouragement:
Today I am on assignment to encourage you to *fear not.* Don't you worry yourself; just stand your ground. You did nothing wrong, so stop looking for ways to blame yourself. Whatever the situation is that has compassed you during the night, *fear not.* This is not the end of the road for you. It is not your final chapter. You will not die here.

I pray that God will open up the mind of your understanding, that you will see that He is greater than the entire world against you. Your enemy does not have the final say. I pray that God will allow you to see the doors of opportunity that are swung open on your behalf. I pray that you will walk therein and find favor. I pray that the power of the Holy Spirit will remove every scale from your eyes and *immediately give you a changed perspective.*

Be blessed always.

_____
_____
_____
_____
_____

My prayer today:

_____
_____
_____
_____
_____

※

> For God loved the world so much that he gave his one and only Son, so that everyone who believes in him will not perish but have eternal life.
>
> John 3:16 (NLT)

This is probably the most well-known scripture, both in Christendom and the world at large. The good news about Jesus, his coming, life, and death, is the true gospel story that is and will continue to set people free from the bondage of sin.

Belief must be *in* Jesus and not just *on* Him, as many have fallen prey to that folly of the devil. Many hear the gospel, believe it is true, but do nothing about accepting Jesus as their Lord and Savior. They cry excuses of being too young or just wanting to wait until they have accomplished some lifetime goals. That, my friend, is only believing on Jesus. Resting in your hands is the choice of everlasting life. Excuses will only deny you this choice, which is rightly yours, through the gift of Jesus Christ. "What kind of deal is it to get everything you want but lose yourself? What could you ever trade your soul for?" (Matthew 16:26 MSG)

Word of Encouragement:
Don't reject the best gift you will ever receive. Go beyond fears and inhibitions and accept the precious blessing of Jesus Christ into your life. You have within you the power to choose life or death. Choose life.

Be blessed always.

_____
_____
_____
_____
_____

My prayer today:

_____
_____
_____
_____
_____

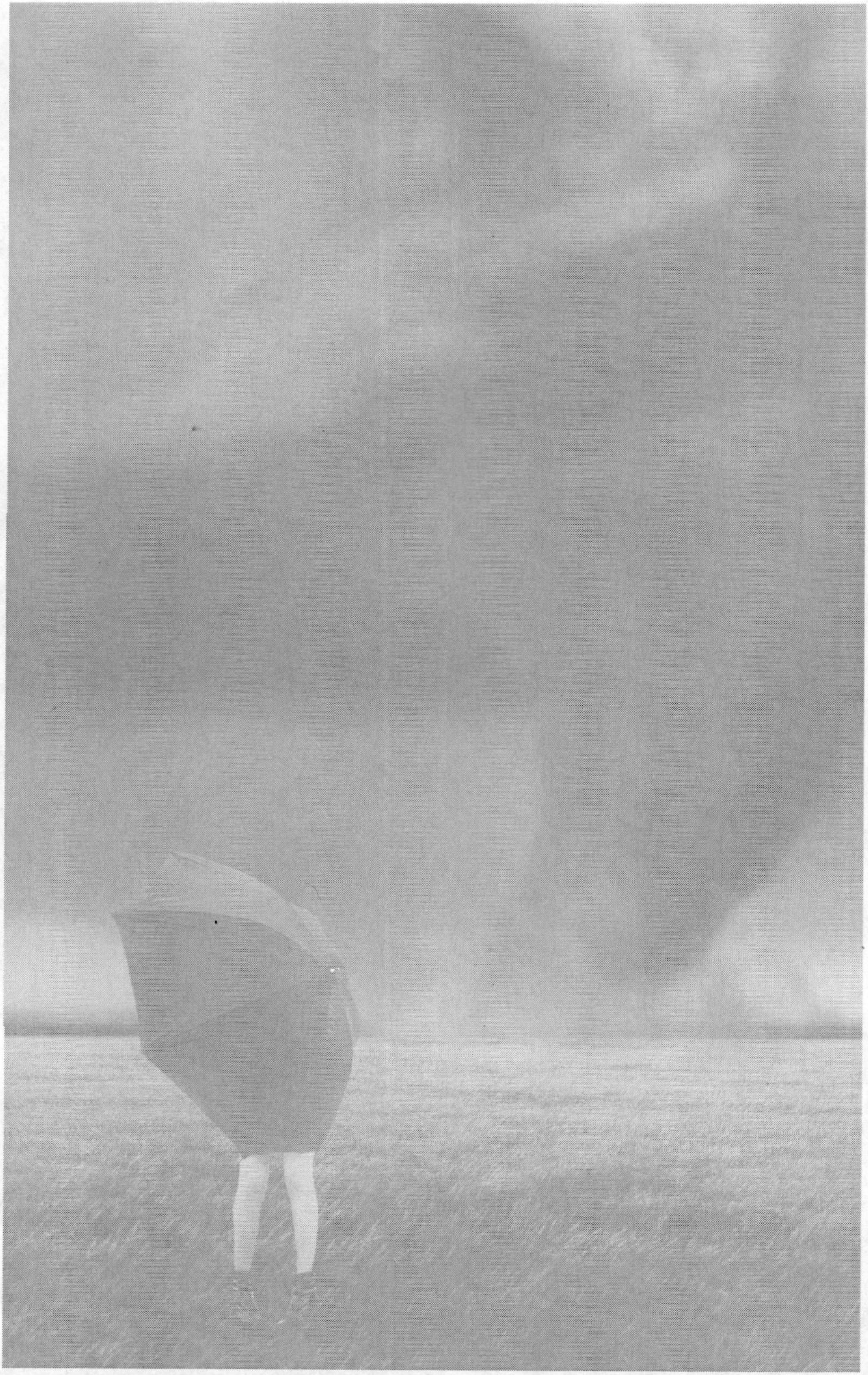

SECTION II
WORRY & ANXIETY

You are what you think. The Word of God in Proverbs 23:7 states "For as he thinketh in his heart so is he" (KJV). Powerful, isn't it? We have the power to change our lives by monitoring our thoughts. Sounds easy? *Not.* In fact, I find that controlling my thoughts is a constant battle, because my thoughts often react to the stimuli of my environment. That's why you can be amongst negative-thinking folks, and before long you find yourself thinking negatively too. As the adage says, "misery loves company."

The apostle Paul helps us out with this dilemma. He gives us a list of things we should focus our thought life on.

> Finally, brethren,
> whatsoever things are true,
> whatsoever things are honest,
> whatsoever things are just,
> whatsoever things are pure,
> whatsoever things are lovely,
> whatsoever things are of good report;
> if there be any virtue, and if there be any praise,
> think on these things.
> Philippians. 4:8 (KJV)

Word of Encouragement:
If you don't like what you are, what you have become, or what you are becoming, change your thought life. And if you are like me and need help, use the above list as a guide-

line. You have choices. You can change. God has given you the power. Work the Word. You will be pleasantly surprised at the wonderful things that God will do.

Be blessed always.

_____
_____
_____
_____
_____

My prayer today:

_____
_____
_____
_____

Today is a brand-new day. One we have never seen before. The possibilities of this day are endless. Miracles await. Blessings await. It is like a blank, new sheet of paper, just waiting for us to write on it. It is a day of second chances, where mistakes can be corrected and new decisions can be made.

What we think today is crucial, because we have the power to make this day what we want it to be. Today we could reunite with a lost relationship. Today we could receive a check in the mail. Today we could receive a clean bill of health. Today we may meet our significant other. Today our walk with God could shift to a new level, and we could find our destiny and purpose.

Today could be the first day of the best days of your life. Think about it. Speak it out. Feel the energy of it revitalize your soul. Shake off the negativity that wants to imprison your day. Kick gloom and doom to the curbside. Tell failure you've had your last dance. Let misery go find itself some new company. Close the door to unsettling thoughts and lingering questions that comes to torment you. Today is the day to walk in agreement with the Word of God.

> The LORD is my shepherd; I shall not want.
> He maketh me to lie down in green pastures:
> he leadeth me beside the still waters. He restoreth my soul: he leadeth me in the paths of righteousness for his name's sake. Yea, though I walk through the valley of the shadow of death, I will fear no evil: for thou art with me; thy rod and thy staff they comfort me. Thou preparest a table before me in the presence of mine enemies: thou anointest my head with oil; my cup runneth over. Surely goodness and mercy shall follow me all the days of my life: and I will dwell in the house of the LORD for ever.
>
> Psalm 23 (KJV)

Be blessed always.

_____
_____
_____
_____

My prayer today:

_____
_____
_____
_____

※

Let the people praise thee, O God; let all the people praise thee"

(Psalm 67:3 KJV).

It's easier to praise God when everything is going fine. When all of our prayers are answered and blessings are flowing like a river. It gets harder to do when all hell is breaking loose and you are gasping for breath. But praising God is not an optional thing. Regardless of how we feel or what it looks like, God is good, and He is worthy to be praised!

Praise operates in the same way fuel works for our cars. We may have the most expensive, latest model, and the fastest car parked in our garage, but if the gas tank is empty, we are going nowhere. With all its horsepower, brilliant interior designs, and technical savvy, the car is practically useless in performing what it was created to do without some form of fuel to get it moving. That why we get so concerned when the price of petroleum escalates, because we know that if we cannot fill up at the pump, the inconvenience would only be a part of our problem. The economy itself would come to stretching halt.

We need to praise in order to survive. It fills us up and keeps us moving. If we don't move then we become stagnant and eventually die. With all our academics accolades, gifts and abilities, money in the bank, family lineages, and importance, we cannot really be useful until we begin to praise God. That's why you will hear folks who seem to have everything—money, family, skills, etc.—still say they have a void that cannot be filled. God created us with praise in mind.

Word of Encouragement:
So today, whether you are living on the mountaintop and feel like you could conquer the world, or you are stranded in the valley and feel like death is closing in on you, praise God today. Praise will elevate your mind and release the grip of despair from you. There is not a situation that you cannot praise your way out of. Why don't you open up your mouth and just praise God today? I promise you, the benefits for you will be greater than you can even imagine.

"Let every thing that hath breath praise the LORD. Praise ye the LORD" (Psalm 150:6 KJV).

Be blessed always.

_____
_____
_____
_____

My prayer today:

_____
_____
_____
_____

※

> If God is for us, who can be against us?
> Romans 8:31(KJV)

I feel excited every time I read this scripture. Why? Because I understand that God is for me. *Awesome!* I have the King of kings, Creator of the universe, actively working on my behalf. Reflecting on this fact, it seems silly for me to be overly concerned about what the enemy is *trying* to do, because God is for me. But exactly what does this mean? To me it means that He is intentionally in favor of my well-being. In layman terms it means: he's got my back.

I want to speak to the person who has been weathering the storms for a long time. You are frustrated and feel defeated. You have been hanging on for a while, waiting for your situation to change, but nothing has happened. You have doubts crawling in the closets of your mind that you are afraid to open. You want to hold on to your faith, but you can feel yourself slipping. You are hoping against hope, but you do not understand why it is taking so long.

Word of Encouragement:
God sends me with a word for you. He wants you to know that He has not forgotten about you. He hears your every cry, and He knows just how you feel. He understands your heart's desires, and He is aware of how difficult it has been for you. But He wants you to trust Him and trust His words. There is nothing or no one that He is going to allow to snatch you from His hands. And He is not going to let you fail or fall. He is holding you, even right now, as you are too weak to carry yourself. Hold on. Cry if you must, but hold on. It will get better. God's purpose in your life will be established. He is your Father, and He cares for you.

Ask yourself the question: *If God is for me, who can stand against me?*

Be blessed always.

_____
_____
_____
_____
_____

My prayer today:

_____
_____
_____
_____
_____

※

This is no news: the global market is going through a slump, and it has created a financial crisis within the world economy. In America we are seeing more foreclosure of homes, unemployment levels rise, people losing money from their retirement funds, and the list goes on.

The question asked is: how will this impact me personally? From my experience, Christians for the most part are known to get extreme in cases of crisis. On the one hand, they hide their heads in the proverbial sand, spiritualize the whole situation, and act as if all that is going on is none of their concern. On the other hand, they act all carnal, lose their faith, and start living and walking in fear. Now is not the time to do either, but rather we must endeavor to be levelheaded—balancing our feelings and our knowledge. The apostle Paul calls it having "a sound mind."

"For God hath not given us the spirit of fear; but of power, and of love, and of a sound mind" (2 Timothy 1:7 KJV).

It was while I was watching the newscast and hearing, for the umpteenth time, the headlines about the "financial crisis" that the LORD spoke to me powerfully. He drew my mind to His words written in St. John 14:1 (KJV): "Let not your hearts be troubled: ye believe in God, believe also in me." The word *heart* is used in scriptures to indicate many attitudes of the mind. In Jeremiah 17:9, the heart is described as being deceitful. My Bible dictionary tells me this means "it will lead us astray by its feelings and its attitudes so that we must not trust in our own desires, but rather be led by the Word of God." You see, in all this mayhem, constantly watching and rehearsing in my mind about the turmoil—present and impending—I was slowly becoming apprehensive about my future. How safe was it? Did it make sense to continue going to school, or should I just quit now? Would I lose my house? What kind of future would my children have? As the questions bombarded my mind, I realized I had let my heart become involved, and it was slowly deceiving me. I was committing the cardinal sin, I was worried about a future—one I had no control over—and doubting God's divine authority over every area in my life—past, present, and future.

Word of Encouragement:
God is still in control. He never changes, and He is still speaking to you as He did to His disciples, thousands of years ago: "Do not let your hearts be troubled. Trust in God, trust also in me" (John 14:1, NIV).

Be blessed always.

_____
_____
_____
_____

My prayer today:

_____
_____
_____
_____

※

Samson's birth was miraculous. Born to an otherwise barren woman after she had an angelic appearance, his primary earthly purpose was to deliver the children of Israel from under the cruel rule of the Philistines. Read his account in Judges 13. The task was simple enough, and like all God-given missions there were restrictions to maintaining the flow of anointing needed to succeed. "No razor to be used on his head" (Judges 13:5 KJV) was the clear instruction given to his mother. Jesus tells us: "for my yoke is easy and my burden is light" (Matthew 11:30 KJV).

I read once that there are three things all Christians have in common: an assignment, an adversary, and an anointing. All three exists codependently of each other. If you have no assignment, you would have no anointing, and no adversary would be there to fight you. In other words if you find the *adversary* (devil) on your case, then he is there only because you have an *assignment,* and God always gives the *anointing* needed for what He has assigned to you. *Think about that!*

I've had times when the devil is fighting me so much, and frankly I don't feel like I am doing anything major to warrant this. But I have found out that the enemy knows the value of my assignment and anointing, even if I am clueless to its worth.

Samson got distracted from his assignment, and the enemy came in for the kill. He made the grave mistake of believing that the anointing would always be there whenever he needed it. *Absolutely not!* He found himself blind and a servant to the people he was born to conquer. LORD, have mercy! Staying on target with your God-given assignment is crucial to your very existence. I am glad Samson's story did not end at this point of his life. He regained sight—though not physically—of his purpose and, in his final hour, was triumphant in killing more Philistines in death than in life.

Word of Encouragement:
Do not belittle whatever assignment God has given you. What God invites you to do will always be greater than you are. Don't worry about it. He will give you the sustaining power to do it. Remember, it is not over until God says it is.

Be blessed always.

_____
_____
_____
_____
_____

My prayer today:

_____
_____
_____
_____

※

"The heights by great men reached and kept, were not obtained by sudden flight. But they, while their companions slept, were toiling upward in the night" (Henry Wadsworth Longfellow). I learned this idiom when I was a little girl. I can remember my teacher having us repeat it at school just before the day's lesson, and it was instilled in me since then that hard work comes with rewards, and if you did nothing, nothing is what you would have. This concept is not new, however, and the principles are taken from scriptures. King Solomon penned these words thousands of years before.

> Go to the ant, thou sluggard; consider her ways, and be wise: Which having no guide, overseer, or ruler; provideth her meat in the summer, and gathereth her food in the harvest. How long wilt thou sleep, O sluggard? When wilt thou arise out of thy sleep? Yet a little sleep, a little slumber, a little folding of the hands to sleep: So shall thy poverty come as one that travelleth, and thy want as an armed man.
> Proverbs 6:6–11 (KJV)

You cannot deny that the economy is in a rough spot, and many of us are feeling the tightness of it. Even if we would like to turn a blind eye to the situation, high prices are rising up and giving a good slap in the face, waking us to the reality that we cannot just sit and do nothing. One of the many blessings God gave us is the gift of creativity. We have the ability within us to be resourceful and to do more than we are presently doing.

I am sure we've all observed an ant carrying a load, twice, even thrice, its size. What a wonder to see! And they do not die or become crushed by the load they carry. They work tirelessly and save while they can. I want to declare this is not the time to be wasting anything—time, money, or gifting. Now is the time to get up and use all that God has given us. No, we will not wait for handouts, we will not sit and pout, and we will not get depressed. We will work. Maybe this is the opportunity for you to write a new book, start a business, or get a second job.

Word of Encouragement:
If an ant can survive through the seasons of life, so can you. Be prayerful and watchful with what God gives you. Take a tip from the ant and work and save in this season. Don't buy into the enemy's lie that there is nothing you can do. Get up and start doing. As Solomon tells us, poverty is traveling, and one day it will get to your street, and you don't want to be found sleeping. Rather, let it pass your destination because you are busy working.

Be blessed always.

My prayer today:

_____
_____
_____
_____

⥈

I had just gone in for a quick stop to pick up a pastry item when I saw it. The customer next to me was getting a serving of "jerk chicken," and my eyes caught a glimpse of his plate. It looked delicious and smelled divine. I had no time to wait, but I made up in my mind that I would have me some soon. For two days all I could think about was getting back to the store to get some of what I had seen.

Watch your eyes; watch your eyes, what they see! While having the "jerk chicken" is not bad in itself, if I allow my desire to germinate, soon it will control me, and I may end up buying more than I really need.

I am reminded of King David, whose eyes got him into a lot of trouble with his family, his kingdom, and ultimately with his God. The Bible tells that one day, while his men were in the midst of battle with the Ammonites, David was walking on top of his roof when he saw a lovely married woman, Bathsheba, bathing. His eyes caught a glimpse of her beauty, and shortly after David made up in his mind to have her. This is perhaps one of the most tragic periods in David's life. He went from committing adultery, to trying a cover up scheme to hide a pregnancy, and escalated to the murdering of the Bathsheba's husband. Read his account in 2 Samuel 11.

The Apostle John warns us not to love the world or its system. He says "For all that is in the world—the lust of the flesh, the lust of the eyes and the pride of live- is not of the Father but is of the world" (1 John 2:16 KJV).

So what had gotten you so frustrated today? Could it be that your eyes had trapped you into lusting for stuff you are not even ready for, and now you are upset because it seems like God is not moving as fast you want Him to? Has this world sucked you in until you have forgotten that you are a mere pilgrim passing through? I like the way James says it. He says:

> Let no one say when he is tempted, "I am tempted by God," for God cannot be tempted by evil nor does He Himself tempt anyone. But each one is tempted when he is drawn away by his own desires and enticed. Then, when desire has conceived, it gives birth to sin; and sin, when it is full-grown, brings forth death.
>
> James 1:13–14 (KJV)

Word of Encouragement:
Take your eyes off the affairs of this world and center them on the only One who is consistent and reliable. You can trust God. With all your heart, soul, and mind. He is able to keep you from falling for the snares of the enemy. Watch your eyes; watch your eyes!

Be blessed always.

_____
_____
_____
_____

My prayer today:

_____
_____
_____
_____

※

I am a firm believer that God created us on purpose and with purpose. To think that a God so meticulous and powerful would create us with no goals in mind is inconceivable. We only have to look at our bodies and see the splendor of creation. It was David who put it in perspective. "I will praise thee; for I am fearfully and wonderfully made" (Psalm 139:14 KJV).

It would be unjust for God to require us to be good stewards if he had not assigned us with something to take care of. Jesus gave a parable in Matthew 25 about a man who traveled to another country and left his property in the hands of his servants to take care of. He gave them five, two, and one talents (a sum of money), according to each ability to manage. After a while the man came home, and each servant gave an account of what he had done with the talent given. The servants, who had received five and two talents invested it and gained a one-hundred percent return of five and two additional talents respectively. They both received commendations and promotions from their employer for being faithful stewards of what they had received. The servant who received the one talent, however, buried his talent, and he was rebuked by his employer and eventually lost his job. I pray God that never happens to me!

We owe it to ourselves to find out what our *real* purpose is. It is only when we are walking in our God-given purpose that true fulfillment can be experienced. The world system has bombarded our thinking into believing that fulfillment is to be found at the end of a successful corporate career, a huge bank account, or a big house on the hill. Even the church, whose kingdom is *not* in this world and standards are *not* set by this system, is caught up in the frenzy to "keep up with the Joneses."

Word of Encouragement:
God has given you exactly what you need to be fulfilled in this life. He had assigned you as steward over your life and in return He is expecting a one hundred percent rate of success. To live below that which God has purposed for you would be equivalent to the servant who buried his talent. Sometimes you'll forget who you are and to whom

you belong. Consequently, you'll bring to your life unnecessary stress and worry. Paul gave the saints in Philippi a golden nugget that you should strive to attain. He said in Philippians 4:11, "for I have learned, in whatsoever state I am, therewith to be content" (KJV). That's it. Contentment. When you walk in purpose, you'll experience true contentment.

Be blessed always.

_____

_____

_____

_____

My prayer today:

_____

_____

_____

_____

I like to do a project from start to finish. This is why I enjoy writing and directing drama plays. I like to see thoughts evolve into words and watch those words take life with action. Coordinating all the elements involved and seeing them come together reminds me of watching my brother work on his car engine. He is a mechanic, and he would take the engine of his car apart to fix one thing or another; and the carport would be filled with all these pieces. I remember looking in amazement, wondering if he would be able to put the engine back together. And sure enough, after several days of him tinkering and cleaning, I would go look, and the car would be up and running, and all the parts would be back in place.

That's how I feel sometimes about my life. I am somewhere between where God is taking me and where I am now. *Transition.* As God works on me to make me the vessel He knows I should be, I feel like I am that car engine that my brother loves to work on. As God sees the need for "tuning up" in my life, He takes me apart piece by piece to get to whatever "hindrance" is present. *I don't feel good when this happens. I feel like I am losing it. I feel out of control. I feel like I will never be the same again. I secretly wonder if God really knows what....*

Yet Paul reminds me that I can have confidence that God will finish the work he has started in my life. "Being confident of this very thing, that he which hath begun a good work in you will perform it until the day of Jesus Christ" (Philippians 1:6 KJV). That even though I may feel tossed about and may be going through a lot of prodding and cleaning, God has my best interest at heart. Songwriter James Cleveland sings, "Please be patient with me, God is not through with me yet, when God gets through with me, I shall come forth like pure gold."

Word of Encouragement:
If you are in transition right now, and you can see the hand of God just taking you apart bit by bit, don't panic! He may need to clean away malice, pride, lust, greed, jealousy, low self-esteem, insecurities, and covetousness to get your engine in top shape for the journey ahead. God is faithful, and what He has started He will complete.

Be blessed always.

_____
_____
_____
_____
_____

My prayer today:

_____
_____
_____
_____
_____

∞

I thank God daily for His grace—undeserving favor—toward me. I was born and raised in the church, but it still took me a long time to really grasp the notion of God's grace. Not because I had not sinned nor believed myself righteous but because I was not as exposed to practicing sin as some were. You may say in some ways my life was sheltered. I never really thought about it until one day a teenager whom I was mentoring asked me this question. She asked, "Do you have to be a hardcore sinner for God to bless and use you?" I was taken aback by the question. I then probed for more information because I wanted to know where this was coming from. She then told me that all the major telepreachers had some story of drugs/abuse/sexual sins in their lives, which they displayed as the reason for their great anointing. She wanted to be mighty for God but was worried that she would have to do one of these things to get noticed in His kingdom. Oh, the mind of a teenager!

This is when it hit me about God's grace. How awesome it is! The songwriter calls it "amazing grace." God's grace is incredible, almost unbelievable. To comprehend God's grace, you have to look at who God is. God is holy, spotless, glorious, all-powerful, and all knowing. When the Prophet Isaiah saw God in his splendor, he cried out, "Woe is me, for I am undone; because I am a man of unclean lips, and I dwell in the midst of a people of unclean lips: for mine eyes have seen the King, the Lord of hosts" (Isaiah 6:3 KJV). It is this same God who reaches down through time to "dwell" among corruptible human flesh, chooses to die on their behalf for their sins, and still chooses to extend His favor toward them that they may prosper and not perish. Paul says to us, "For by grace are ye saved through faith; and that not of yourselves: it is the gift of God" (Ephesians 2:8 KJV).

So back to the teenager's question. While I profoundly told her that the enemy who had a hidden agenda to destroy her was distorting her thinking, I shared with her the magnitude of the amazing grace of God. His grace is a gift to us, and it is such a wonderful gift that even the vilest of sinners has the same access to it. Thank You, Jesus, for Your grace.

Word of Encouragement:
God's grace is enough for you. Think about it. God has given you His unmerited favor and there is nothing the devil can do about it. You ought to want to shout because justice had to bypass you when grace stood in your stead. Enjoy the grace of God.

Be blessed always.

_____
_____
_____
_____

My prayer today:

_____
_____
_____
_____

◈

It can be difficult to forgive someone who has done you wrong. When your trust is betrayed and you feel as if someone had deliberately taken advantage of your Christianity, forgiving can be hard. Now forgiving a stranger is one thing, but forgiving someone whom you consider a friend is a different playing field. David puts it this way: "For it was not an enemy that reproached me; then I could have borne it: neither was it he that hated me that did magnify himself against me; then I would have hid myself from him" (Psalms 55:12 KJV).

Forgiveness is not a "gray area" for God. This is not one of those things that we can have a round table discussion about and research Greek/Hebrew translations to find an understanding about what the author meant in the content of the scripture written at the time. No. Forgiveness for God is a *must*. In English, Hebrew, Greek, Spanish, whatever language—it is not optional.

Jesus says, "But if ye forgive not men their trespasses, neither will your Father forgive your trespasses" (Matthew 6:15 (KJV). Whew! Take a deep breath and read that again.

I know you may have questions for God at this point. What about the coworker who tried to slander you in order to get the promotion at work? The answer is "yes." What about the spouse that walked out on you and the kids, bills unpaid, and left you on the street? The answer is still "yes." Lord, what about the friend who told a lie to me and caused me to lose important relationships and years of productivity? The Lord is still saying, "Yes, you must forgive."

Word of Encouragement:
Forgiveness is not an open season for others to abuse you and get away with it. No! God knows that in this lifetime offenses will come, but learning to forgive releases you of the pain and the hurt. It shuts the door to bitterness and allows God's healing to take place in your life. He is a just God, and He promises you that if you but trust Him, He will not give you more than you can bear.

Be blessed always.

_____
_____
_____
_____

My prayer today:

_____
_____
_____
_____

***

For three and a half years, Jesus walked in ministry on this earth and had a relationship with twelve men, known as his disciples. He worked miracles in their sight and taught them the Word. They had experiences with Him that no other man in this lifetime ever will. He stretched them and challenged them beyond their comfort zones, and then it was time for His death. He forewarned them about what would happen and even told Peter he would deny Him. Yet I am always amazed at what happened when the rubber finally met the road. "And they all forsook him, and fled" (Mark 14:50 KJV).

I am not lofty to believe that I am any different from the disciples. After walking for many years with the LORD, I still struggle and stumble at His Words. There is never a day that I feel like I don't need His guidance or direction. And I am not volunteering frontline service to be the next Job. No, I would prefer to just have sunshine all the time, even though it may not be good for me. Maybe I am selfish...maybe I am just human. But I would love to have all my prayers answers before I am even finished praying.

Word of Encouragement:
God knows you are human, and yes, He knows you are His child. So if you feel like you have forsaken Him and fled from His presence, don't worry. He is beckoning for you to return. His arms are open wide as He awaits you. He is only a prayer away and closer than you believe. Come back to Him and begin walking again.

> But his father said to the servants, 'Quick! Bring the finest robe in the house and put it on him. Get a ring for his finger and sandals for his feet. And kill the calf we have been fattening. We must celebrate with a feast, for this son of mine was dead and has now returned to life. He was lost, but now he is found.' So the party began.
>
> Luke 15:22–24 (NLT)

Thank God the disciples did not stay away. Later they became the apostles of the gospel, and God used them mightily.

Be blessed always.

_____

_____

_____

_____

_____

My prayer today:

_____

_____

_____

_____

God takes obedience seriously. When he instructs us, He expects us to do just what He says. This is not to be confused with the behavior of a dictator who rules without concerns for his subjects. God is sovereign, and He governs our lives from the platform of love and mercy. As individuals we totally expect obedience from our children and subordinates in the workplace. In today's society *obedience* is not a trendy word. In fact, many cringe at the word and immediately conjure up thoughts of the ills of slavery. Obedience to God is acknowledging His sovereignty and giving Him honor and trust. *It is not an option.*

I read a story once about a young minister who was filled with zeal about working for the Lord. He had just finished the seminary, and he was ready to save the world for Jesus. His thoughts were that the world was too small a place for both him and the devil. After graduation God sent him to be the pastor of a small church in a rural village. He was devastated. He pleaded with God to remove him from these small-minded people and use him on a big scale to save the nations. After three years with this small congregation, God told him he was more interested in his obedience to Him than any work he could do. God used this first assignment to teach this young pastor the importance of obedience.

Walking in obedience daily can be challenging. Personally, I have questioned God when I could not quite trace His steps. I tell myself I am not willfully disobedient, that I am just getting clarity, but deep down I know this is not true. When God's will conflicts with my desires, I often falter. Thank God I am learning more each day to trust Him, and the LORD had to teach me a few lessons like that young pastor. Make no mistake, God hates our disobedience. God told King Saul through the prophet Samuel, "Behold, to obey is better than sacrifice, and to hearken than the fat of rams" (1 Samuel 15:22 KJV). When King Saul disobeyed God's commandment regarding the children of Amalekites, God rejected his kingship. "For rebellion is as the sin of witchcraft, and stubbornness is as iniquity and idolatry. Because thou hast rejected the word of the LORD, he hath also rejected thee from being king" (1 Samuel 15:23 KJV).

Word of Encouragement:
Walk in obedience. The temptation to just tune God out may be something you are struggling with, but I beg you to resist the urge. Running away as an alternative to being obedient to God will never get you to a place of fulfillment and destiny. God knows what is best for you, even when you cannot see or understand. Trust Him regardless. He will never fail. He will never leave you nor forsake you.

Be blessed always.

_____
_____
_____
_____

My prayer today:

_____
_____
_____
_____

Showers of Blessings!
As I meditated I heard in my spirit "an abundance of rain." My mind was brought to the scriptures during the time in the history of Israel when they were worshipping idols and God had stopped the rain for over three years. God used the Prophet Elijah to bring the people to a decision about his Sovereignty and to destroy all the false prophets of Baal. God promised He would send rain. "And Elijah said unto Ahab, Get thee up, eat and drink; for there is a sound of abundance of rain" (1 Kings 18:41 KJV).

This is what the LORD quickened my spirit to tell you today:

There is an abundance of blessings coming your way. Unexpected Blessings. Undeserved Blessings. Blessings without reservation that no man can hinder. For I have opened up the floodgates of heaven on your behalf, and already the clouds have gathered. I have shut every door that the enemy wanted to open and have opened doors that none can shut.
I have heard your cries and have seen that you had trusted me in the face of adversity. Your faith had been strengthened, and you had looked expectantly to me. Nothing you did missed my attention, even when you thought my silence meant my disapproval.
Today your wait is over. Your cup will overflow with the blessings I have in store for you. Pressed down and running over, shall it overtake you. Blessings of Merit. Blessings that adds no sorrow. Blessings from my hand.
So dry your tears and set your affairs in order. Make room to receive from me what I have for you. Do not be afraid to receive from me. It is my good pleasure that you enjoy what I have given you.

Be blessed always.

_____

_____

_____

_____

My prayer today:

_____

_____

_____

_____

⚭

God wants us to prosper. Here on this physical side of life, not only in the eternal by and by. "Beloved, I wish above all things that thou mayest prosper and be in health, even as thy soul prospereth" (3 John 1:2 KJV). He wants us to prosper in totality—body, soul, and spirit—and enjoy this prosperity in all areas of our lives.

For many, finding the dividing lines between greed and prosperity can be difficult. Self-indulgence for many is the driving force behind getting more and more. Some folks will not even offer you a cup of water without a price attach to it. Even in the church, greed is often hidden under carefully labeled words like *fellowshipping* and *socializing* when, in fact, "networking" for the next monetary gain is the real agenda. You may have heard the term "fleecing the flock." Unfortunately many leaders are guilty of using their authoritative influence to strip a congregation of money or other property unjustly, especially by trickery.

I often wonder how much is too much. I am sometimes surprised by the reactions of others when I tell them that God is not the only one that can give what seems like a blessing. The devil and the worldly system are also able to offer great attractive packages, which will only lead to sorrow. King Solomon gives great words of wisdom to measure our prosperity by. "The blessing of the Lord, it maketh rich, and he addeth no sorrow with it" (Proverbs 10:22 KJV). It is extremely important that we allow the Holy Spirit to lead and direct us daily. He is our teacher, and, if we allow Him, He will shine the light so we can see clearly before we walk into danger.

Word of Encouragement:
Purpose in your mind to prosper. Live righteously, give generously, eat healthy, exercise daily, and feed your spirit on the Word of God. Ask God to help you to balance your life so that on this earth you may benefit from the prosperity He has designed for you and from the reward He has for you in heaven.

Be blessed always.

_____
_____
_____
_____

My prayer today:

_____
_____
_____
_____

※

Some days I feel so empty. Yet I have learned that my feelings are not stable enough for me to rely on them. If I do, they will constantly take me on a roller-coaster ride. The only consistency I have in this life is the Word of God. It is the only sure foundation on which I can stand. Everything else around me is just sinking sand—temporalities that will soon fade away.

Take the state of the world's economy, for example. There is so much negativity about it these days. Even the saints of God are getting perturbed and "jumpy" about the failing economy. People are losing jobs, homes, and cars, and families are under a lot of pressure to survive. Marriages are failing. Good mentors and role models are hard to find. Leaders are folding under scrutiny, and even many preachers are not living the gospel that they prophesy. It's end times, y'all.

Thank God a higher authority governs us. We are not relying on the economy, a political party, a person, or even ourselves. Instead, we are standing on every promise that God has given us in His Word. I refuse to held hostage by the negative reports. If God is unable to deliver me, what can man do? I have decided to free myself with the power of God's Word. "For the word of God is quick, powerful, and sharper than any twoedged sword, piercing even to the dividing asunder of soul and spirit, and of the joints and marrow, and is a discerner of the thoughts and intents of the heart" (Hebrews 4:12 KJV).

Word of Encouragement:
Keep your focus on Jesus Christ and hold on to the promises He has given you. The answer is only in Him. He loves you too much to let you fail, and He already has a great investment in you. You will win.

Be blessed always.

_____
_____
_____
_____
_____

My prayer today:

_____
_____
_____
_____

⚭

> Do not fret because of evildoers; Be not envious toward wrongdoers.
>
> Psalm 37:1 (nas)

In these tough times, the child of God is faced with difficult decisions in upholding his or her faith and walking in integrity. The temptation is present to be as dishonest as the next person, and the battle of the mind is definitely raging. Evildoers *seemingly* live the easy life, while the saint of God continues to struggle to make ends meet.

> It is too common for believers in their hours of adversity to think themselves harshly dealt with when they see persons utterly destitute of religion and honesty, rejoicing in abundant prosperity. Nature is very apt to kindle a fire of jealousy when it sees lawbreakers riding on horses, and obedient subjects walking in the mire.
> (Bible Commentaries: The Treasury of David)

Word of Encouragement:
To fret is "to worry, to have the heartburn, to fume, to become vexed." God wants to remind you not to worry about what is going on around you. Take your focus from the people and events and turn your attention to Him alone. Do what is right always, even in the face of unpleasant consequences. Be assured that good will overcome evil, and God will always prevail. Call on the peace of God to surround you when the situation seems overwhelming. Hold on to every promise that you have received from the Lord, knowing that God will uphold with His right hand and you will not fall. Take time to pray. This will give you the fuel you need to continue the journey, because you cannot afford to give up now. Do not harbor resentment toward anyone, even those trying to use you, as this will make you sick. Do not compromise the anointing on your life; it is too valuable to lose to anyone and for anything.

When it gets too much to handle, God will make a way of escape; so instead of running away, look for it. Meditate daily on the Word. Gain inner strength to fight your battles. Live only one day at a time. Tomorrow is not promised, and tomorrow will speak for itself. When you have done your best, be satisfied with it. Do not burden yourself with exaggerated, unrealistic expectations. Be flexible. God is the Potter, and you are the clay. He will mold you into what He has planned for you. Connect with people in a real way. Be genuine with friends and be cautious with foes. Forgive yourself. Forgive others. Know this: there are things in this life that are out of your control, but you serve a limitless God, with omnipotent power and a love for you that passes all human understanding. He is the Alpha-Omega, beginning and ending. Get yourself in His grace. Secure your life under His Wings.

> Wait on the LORD, and keep his way, and he shall exalt thee to inherit the land: when the wicked are cut off, thou shalt see it. I have seen the wicked in great power, and spreading himself like a green bay tree. Yet he passed away, and, lo, he was not: yea, I sought him, but he could not be found.
> Psalm 37:34–36 (NAS)

Be blessed always.

_____
_____
_____
_____

My prayer today:

_____
_____
_____
_____

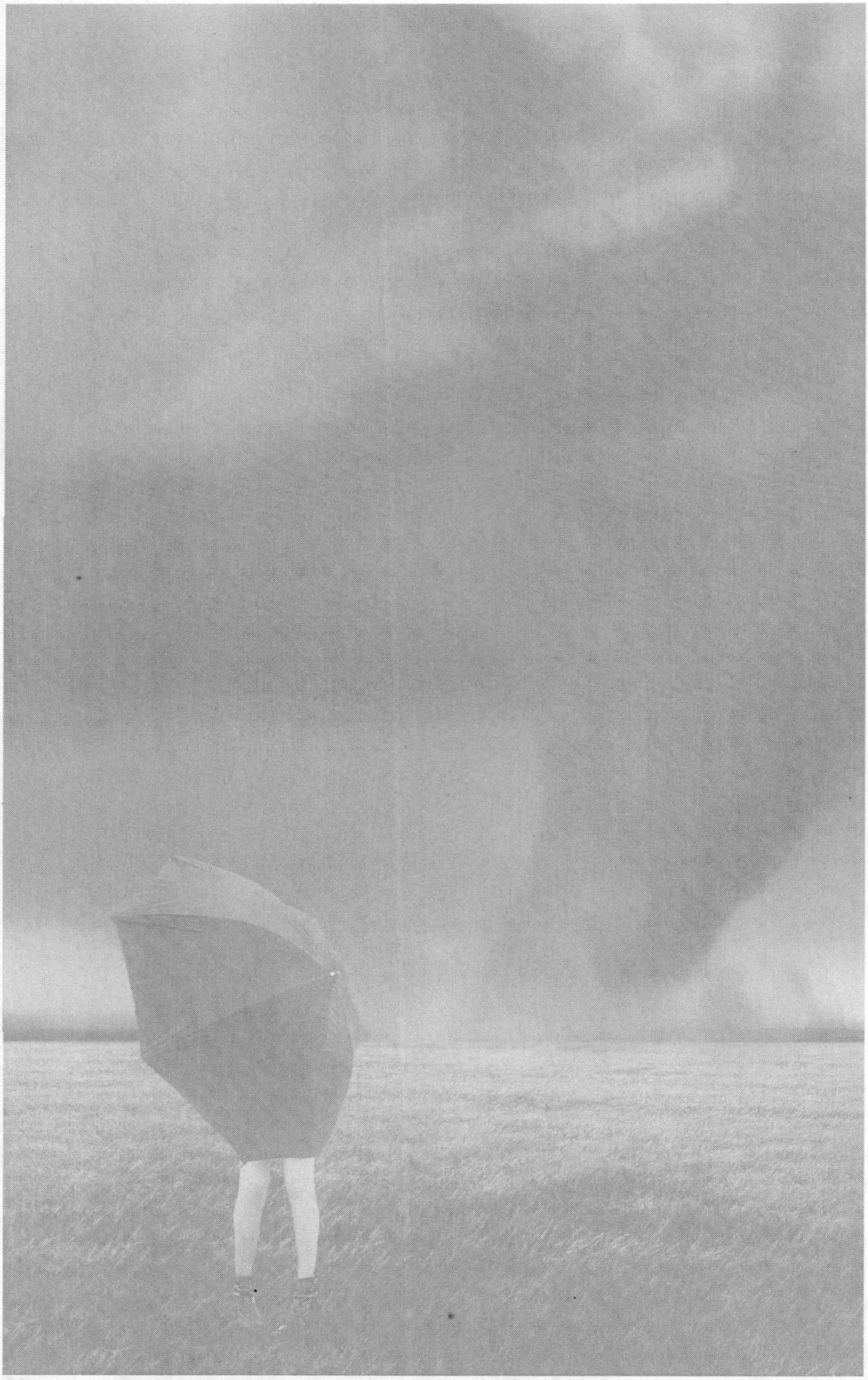

SECTION III
FRUSTRATION & DISAPPOINTMENT

I want to speak today to those who are at the point of giving up. You have weighed your options and have considered and reconsidered it. You have prayed, but it seems like heaven is silent, and you have read the word of God but no answer is coming. In your mind you have resolved to give up on the matter. To give up on your walk with God, your marriage, your friends, even life itself.

The Bible tells of a time in the life of Israel when they disobeyed God and were held captive by the Midianites. The enemy took everything from them, including food, and they were starving because of this. "And Israel was greatly impoverished because of the Midianites; and the children of Israel cried unto the LORD" (Judges 6:6). The dictionary gives the meaning of the word *impoverish* as "to cause somebody or something to be poor or poorer (often passive)." Right now this is what has happened to your spirit. You have become weary in the battle. Don't be alarmed, because this happens to the best of us. We are but human, and there is no doubt that we need the LORD. This does not mean you did anything wrong or that your motives were incorrect. Crying out to the LORD is not a sign of weakness but the testing of your faith. It takes courage to stand in the midst of uncertainty. You are not a failure to God; neither can you do anything that would surprise Him. He is not caught off guard by your actions or your improvised state of mind. God always hears the cry of His children. *Always.* In this impoverished Israel, God found one man, Gideon, hiding in a winepress from the Midianites, threading wheat for food. "And the angel of the LORD appeared unto him, and said unto him, The LORD is with thee, thou mighty man of valour" (Judges 6:12 KJV). To put it mildly, Gideon was taken aback by the greeting he received. In Gideon's mind he did not qualify for such accolades, but, like Gideon, when God speaks to us, He calls us as He sees us, not in the state that we are currently in. You may feel improvised, but, in reality, in God you are rich. You may feel weak, but in Him you are strong.

Word of Encouragement:
Do not give up. God is with you. He will make a way of escape for you. Just keep on living. Sure it is a hard place to be at, but I believe that God will see you through. Speak words of life to yourself. You have the ability to do more than you think. God is enabling you to be victorious in all your endeavors.

Be blessed always.

_____
_____
_____
_____

My prayer today:

_____
_____
_____
_____

Psalm 42

"As the hart panteth after the water brooks, so panteth my soul after thee, O God."

Lord, I am like a deer in the deep of the woods, looking for a water hole. I have traveled for miles, and every pond I have found is dry. My desire for you, Lord, is great. I am weary from the exhaustion of the heat.

"My soul thirsteth for God, for the living God: when shall I come and appear before God?"

Lord, I am so thirsty for you. I have tried a number of substitutes, but it only increased my longing for you even more. I am tired of the fakeness that I find and the pretentiousness that surrounds. I am dry within, and nothing has quenched me. I don't want a form of godliness. I don't want PowerPoint presentations. I don't want eloquent orators. I want the true and living God. I want to see and experience the dynamite power of the Holy Ghost.

"My tears have been my meat day and night, while they continually say unto me, Where is thy God?"

Lord, I am crying for you. My appetite is gone wry because of this. I am not hungry for food; I am just hungry for you. I am praying and fasting continually, because I need to find you. You told me to seek and I would find, and I am doing just that. Others have noticed my distress and are asking me questions about your whereabouts. They know I am your child and that You love me.

"When I remember these things, I pour out my soul in me: for I had gone with the multitude, I went with them to the house of God, with the voice of joy and praise, with a multitude that kept holyday."

Lord, I reminisce often about you. I think about the days when I was in close relationship with you and I felt so alive. I hate that those days are gone. I miss the sweet fellowship of the saints when they didn't just see me a network contact, but when they were really interested in my soul and my welfare.

"Why art thou cast down, O my soul? and why art thou disquieted in me? hope thou in God: for I shall yet praise him for the help of his countenance."

Lord, help me out of this depressive state. Give me the boldness and the voice again to rejoice in you. Help me to shake this dust of rejection and stand tall in you once again. For I know that I will yet again walk with you in full unity, and our relationship will once again be renewed.

P.S. Lord, I forget to say I Love You!

Be blessed always.

_____
_____
_____
_____

My prayer today:

_____
_____
_____
_____

Have you ever felt like jumping ship? You see a pending shipwreck and decide it may be better to ditch it now. Let's face it: life can be very unfair. Bad things still happen to good people. You may be living for God all your life, walking obediently in His word, and still be the one facing a loss of job, a divorce, a terminal illness, family on drugs, or a jail sentence. Being a child of God does not exempt you from pain, despair, disappointment, folks lying to you, or evil people trying to kill you. You can still be misunderstood, hated, cursed, and abused, even when you have done nothing wrong!

It is at times like these that we feel like walking away. I am reminded of the Apostle Paul when he was being transported by ship to Rome to stand trial for the gospel, and the ship was caught in a storm. For days they were lost, thought they would die, and the soldiers—for fear of death—thought they should abandon ship. But Paul gave them a word of advice. "Paul said to the centurion and to the soldiers, except these abide in the ship, ye cannot be saved" (Act 27:31 KJV).

Now think about it. When our feelings get in the way, we tend to lose sound reasoning. We forget the lessons we have already learned. What good would it have done for them to jump overboard? None. The chances of being hurt outside the ship are greater than within. John Maxwell wrote in his book *Thinking for Change*, "If you will control your thoughts, you will control your feelings." Our thought life is important, because it controls our destiny.

Word of Encouragement:
Stay on board. I know you may feel like running away. But this is not the right decision. You must stay on board. It is the safest place to be. I like the way the story ends. They listened to Paul's advice, and they all made it safely to the shore. "And the rest, some on boards, and some on broken pieces of the ship. And so it came to pass, that they escaped all safe to land" (Acts 27: 44 KJV). You will make it. Just wait and see.

Be blessed always.

_____
_____
_____
_____

My prayer today:

_____
_____
_____
_____

※

Just when you thought life could not get any worse, your situation could not be any more complicated, it is. Disappointments are so unsettling. Your expectations are way high, and the let down can be difficult to handle. I am not sure if it is humanly possible to arrive at a stage in life where they just pass without leaving a mark. I have gotten so disappointed over issues until I didn't know how to react. Should I cry, curse, go on a shopping spree, an eating binge, or just quit? In some instances, walking away is not an option. If you are broke, about to lose your house, or you did not get the job after the umpteenth interview, you cannot just stop looking for a job or going to interviews. The domino effect of such actions could be devastating and would only prolong the effects of the disappointment.

The question that pops into my mind during this time is whether or not this is a God testing moment for me. On the one hand, if this is just a test then I need to re-evaluate the situation and see what lessons I need to take away from it. But if this is an attack from the enemy, then I need to reinforce my position and strategically plan how to overcome this battle. We have to keep in mind that just because we are doing everything right it is not a guarantee that we will not still have disappointments. I seek comfort in the word of God written in the book of Romans. "And we know that all things work together for good to those who love God, to those who are called according to His purpose" (Romans 8:28, NKJV). Thank you, Jesus!

Word of Encouragement:
You may not feel it right now, but this too will pass. Resist the urge to distrust God and hold on to the proven fact that He is faithful. Reflect on His goodness to you. Meditate on His love. I know you are in the right place to receive a blessing, and God has a way of working suddenly. He can change your situation. Whatever happens, know this: you are not finished, and your life is not over.

Be blessed always.

_____
_____
_____
_____

My prayer today:

_____
_____
_____
_____

※

I feel like a stepchild, like I am an unwanted member of the family. These were the thoughts racing through my mind all day. Why? I had been praying now for weeks about an issue—which to me was urgent—and here I was another day with no solution. I started to rebuke the negative thought as it kept playing in my head because I knew enough of God's Word to know that this was not true; but deep down in my emotions this was exactly how I felt. It seemed to me that everyone I spoke to was sharing testimonies about how God had answered them about the same matter that I had been agonizing and seeking Him about. I feel like a stepchild. By the end of the day, I was emotionally drained, and I had retreated to a hiding place in my mind where I no longer thought about the issue. Secretly I was getting depressed.

Unanswered prayers. The thing I really love about the LORD is that he will not let us just sit in whatever pit we find ourselves in. It was King David who declared in Psalm 40:1–2

> I waited patiently for the LORD; and he inclined unto me, and heard my cry. He brought me up also out of an horrible pit, out of the miry clay, and set my feet upon a rock, and established my goings.
>
> (KJV)

I got a phone call the next day. From another state, someone was calling with a message that God had given for me. The Word was precise, simple, and profound. "For God is not unrighteous to forget your work and labour of love, which ye have shewed toward his name, in that ye have ministered to the saints, and do minister" (Hebrews 6:10 KJV). Wow! I was floored by the compassion of God.

Word of Encouragement:
You may occasionally go through life by way of the pit, but this is not your final destination. God answers your prayers but often not in the time frame you may wish or the way you may desire. To date I still have the issue unresolved, but I no longer feel pressured or burdened by it. I know that God is working it out, and I am going to be just fine.

How about you today? Do you have *seemingly* unanswered prayers? God makes "pit stops," and He is coming to your rescue.

Be blessed always.

_____
_____
_____
_____

My prayer today:

_____
_____
_____
_____

I feel the need to speak to someone today who is feeling really frustrated and discouraged. Things have not been going your way. You think it could never get worse, but you were proven wrong. You feel like your faith is slipping, like you are on a slippery slope that is heading for the bottom of nowhere at rapid speed. You are not sure how you got to this point in your life, what wrong turn you made. It feels like one day you woke up and had bright sunshine, and then, without warning, dark clouds drifted your way and refused to leave.

Am I speaking to you? You have prayed about it. Still nothing seems to be happening. You have cried and read the scriptures, but God seems to be silent at this time. You have fellowship with the saints, but you feel like you are just going through the motions. The questions in your head are many. You are tempted to return to an old habit you had put off, as the pressure seems to be mounting.

Right now you are not sure who to really talk to. Who will understand? Most people think you have it all. They have no idea about the different masks you wear. Not that you are trying to deceive anyone; it is just a part of the survival gear that you have. But all this is starting to weigh you down, and something is going to have to give.

Am I still speaking to you? If you can identify with this place, then I will tell you, don't worry—you are human. How can I say so? Because I have been there. I have traveled on this road. We all have, and if you haven't yet, you will. The word tells us as humans our days are few and they are "full of trouble" (Job 14:1 KJV).

Word of Encouragement:
Today I want to tell you something you already know. God loves you. He cares too much about you to let this "trouble" destroy you. He promises that He will not give you more than you can bear, so I know you can take it and you will make it. I know right now it may not seem possible, but just hold on. Don't give up. I know quitting may seem like

it is the easy way out. It is not. I beg of you, do not quit. God will bring a sudden change in your life, like a fresh shower of rain after a long drought. "But God put his love on the line for us by offering his Son in sacrificial death while we were of no use whatever to him" (Romans 5:8 MSG).

Be blessed always.

_____
_____
_____
_____

My prayer today:

_____
_____
_____
_____

It is said that insanity is doing the *same* thing over and over and expecting a *different* result. That's comforting to know! Life is a cycle, a wheel of events sequenced in time zones that always repeat itself. It, therefore, means that every year we will experience spring, summer, fall, and winter. It is a given. Yet we get all worked up every time we go through an unpleasant season. *Insanity.* Yes I know winter is harsh, cold, and difficult, but we must be prepared in our minds to face it each time. Guess what? This too shall pass.

Recently I had a difficult issue that I had been trying to resolve for over six months. Every week I did the same thing. I constantly made phone calls, which was very time consuming, yet I was no sooner to getting my problem resolved. Before long I had fallen into the downward spiral of whining, complaining, and murmuring. This was not a good place for me because I was getting irritable each passing day, and I could tell that even my spirit was involved. After a couple more days of wallowing in self-pity and still getting no results, the Lord spoke to me and told me it was time to let it go. I was shocked! I had a genuine problem, so how could I just ignore it and pretend as if everything was okay. Have you ever had one of those moments when you *know* you had to have heard wrong? But God reminded me to keep my focus on what is important and to just keep on living.

He is the same God. He does not change, and I will always get the same results with Him—His everlasting Love.

Word of Encouragement:
So what have you been stressing yourself over and over again about? I know that worrying about it has not brought you closer to a solution. Live in the sanity of God's love.

He is a never-failing friend that will be with you through every season of life. As He speaks to you, prayerfully trust His words and find the peace He is giving to you.

Be blessed always.

_____
_____
_____
_____
_____

My prayer today:

_____
_____
_____
_____

※

I have matured enough to understand that the devil is always plotting, scheming, or warring against me, or rather against my soul. My mind is a constant battlefield as the war between right and wrong is waged. I must confess: I don't always win every battle. I had an argument turned quarrel with my husband the other day, and my thoughts *and speech* were so warped that I was ashamed of myself.

Looking back, I cannot even tell what we were really in contention about. Trivial matters get blown out of proportion, and before we know it we are walking the path of regret.

I take courage in understanding that the devil is already defeated and will not win the war. Jesus guaranteed victory for me on Calvary a long time ago. A battle loss, therefore, does not signal the waving of the white flag. No, I don't have to surrender to a life of defeat because I was unsuccessful. I have choices. I have the word of God. His words tells me

> No weapon that is formed against thee shall prosper; and every tongue that shall rise against thee in judgment thou shalt condemn. This is the heritage of the servants of the LORD, and their righteousness is of me, saith the LORD.
>
> Isaiah 54:17 (KJV)

So I spoke to my husband and reminded him that we have the same enemy, and we should pool our resources and fight against him and not let him fight between us. He agreed. *Whew!*

Word of Encouragement:
Don't give the enemy a foothold in your life. Yes, he may try to terrify you by the many weapons he is displaying, wanting to make a havoc of your life. No weapon shall prosper. That's a promise. Walk with your head up high, and, if you fall, know that you will get back up again. This is your birthright as a child of God.

Be blessed always.

_____
_____
_____
_____

My prayer today:

_____
_____
_____
_____

The phrase "easy come, easy go" even as it relates to spiritual things is normally true. You can mark the person that had to put much effort into reaching some goal in life. Such a one will protect it with everything they have. *Hold on to what you've got.*

If we are not careful, we will discount the things we already have. For all of us there is often a wide gap between our ideal and our actuality. And no one has all ideals in life. There is always some area in our lives that does not quite add up to what we "ideally" think it should be. And just because something is ideal does not mean it is what is best for you. For example, when my children were younger, an "ideal" job for me had less to do with salary but more to do with flexibility of work hours. This allowed me to spend more time with my family, which to me had the greater value. . You must be watchful of the enemy's subtle messages that are sent to undermine your actuality and make you lose what God has ordained for you at this particular phase of your life. *Hold on to what you've got.*

We must endeavor not to lose anything but to hold on to what we have. And yes, we have a lot of valuables that the enemy wants us to lose. Take, for instance, your peace. Irreplaceable. Hold on to it. Safeguard it against every tactic of the enemy. Hold on to your joy. In these tough times when the economy is giving you the roller-coaster ride of your life, keep your joy close beside you. The apostle Paul encourages us to be content, satisfied, at ease in whatever state we find ourselves in. "I am not saying this because I am in need, for I have learned to be content whatever the circumstances" (Philippians 4:11, NIV).

Word of Encouragement:
Hold on to what you've got. If God has given it to you for this season in your life, don't you let it go. Remember how many tears you had to cry, how many devils you had to fight, how many times you had to encourage yourself to get to where you are right now. Take a tighter hold of your faith, family, friends, and finances and walk in the liberty that God has given you.

Be blessed always.

_____
_____
_____
_____

My prayer today:

_____
_____
_____
_____

※

You may remember the Bible's account of the three young Hebrew men—Shadrach, Meshach, and Abednego—who were taken captivity into the land of Babylon during the reign of Nebuchadnezzar. They are not like many who are only believers when in the presence of the saints at church, but even in captivity they stood up for what they believed in. We could certainly take lessons from their pages!

Read Daniel chapter 3. For refusing to obey the practice of idolatry (by bowing to a graven image) they were thrown into a furnace of fire. *Wow!* I don't know about you, but as I read this story, I have to ask the question: why would God allow this to happen when they were doing the right thing? And then I had my "ahhaa" moment! You see, God is a God of purpose, promise, and power.

The crazy thing about living is, we don't always know what is on God's agenda for our lives. *Psst*...And God does not usually send us a memo with a detailed itinerary of what item is up next. Personally I have never heard anyone pray for God to send them through any setbacks, like the death of a loved one, hard financial times, living on the streets, or going without food for days. But it would be foolish for us to believe that we are immune from such tragedies. Can you imagine what was going on in the minds of these young men as they were faced with such a challenging situation?

Make no mistake, they were not superheroes or super saints. I believe they were ordinary people, like you and me, who were willing to risk everything they had—including life—on the basis of their faith in God—one whom they had never seen and who had seemingly forsaken them as they lived in slavery. These men were honest in their response. In my own words, they said, "We don't know if God is going to deliver; He can, but He may chose not to. Either way we are still not going to bow to your graven images." Read verses 17–18.

Word of Encouragement:
Stop trying to explain every "bad" thing away. Sure God is a healer, but what if He chose not to heal you? Will it alter how you believe in Him? This battle is tough, but you are not alone. You have the witnesses of these young men,

cheering you on to victory. Keep this thought in mind: the purpose of God will lead you, the promise of God will hold you, and the power of God will deliver you.

Be blessed always.

_____
_____
_____
_____

My prayer today:

_____
_____
_____
_____

~~~

> "Behold, I am the LORD, the God of all flesh: is there any thing too hard for me?"
> Jeremiah 32:27 (KJV)

What is it you desire from the LORD today? *Think about it.* As I read this scripture I realize that God is challenging my faith and thinking. Many live like paupers in God's kingdom, thinking they are doing the right thing, when in fact they are not. I have even heard saints take the defense that their thinking is that of humility. But how can we possibly justify that God, our Father, is the King of the uNIverse—rich in everything and yet living a life of deficiency that we are not able to influence anyone in our sphere.

Our thinking has got to change. We have to forget some of the "inaccurate" teachings we had received, directly or indirectly. If God is your Father, and you are His child, then what He has, you have. Period.

The gospel's account of the life of Jesus Christ on earth was not one of barely surviving or trying to keep afloat. Christ walked in the authority of the Father at all times, and He exercised power over every demonic force. *News flash!* We have that same authority. We have that same power. I believe the underlying problem is that our thinking needs to be elevated. When we were "adopted" into the family of God and we became new creation in Christ, our position changed, but our thinking is still a bit slow, and we have not yet caught up to our new status.

Word of Encouragement:
God wants you to have all that He destined for you. He is a gracious Father, wanting His children to be victorious just like He is. He is the God of all flesh. He wants you to bring all your cares to Him and ask Him what you desire. Don't be afraid to talk to God. He is not intimated by your concerns. God is still asking this question: is there anything too hard for Me?

Be blessed always.

_____
_____
_____
_____
_____

My prayer today:

_____
_____
_____
_____
_____

I normally set the time on my alarm clock ten minutes ahead so that I have the extra ten-minute window to work in each morning. The problem I am having is that the clock keeps jumping ahead outside of the ten minutes window. I normally wait until it's about thirty minutes ahead (not good when you wake up too early), and then I just patiently reset it to the time that I want.

It got me thinking, *how often we do the right thing in the wrong time?* Not knowing and sensing God's timing can cause us unnecessary confusion. Moses is a prime example from the scriptures of someone who operated "rightly" but outside of the correct timing of God. When he saw the injustices being done to his people and had an opportunity to do something about it, he went ahead and did it. What he thought was a secret (he killed a man and buried him in the sand) backfired when the same people he was trying to help threatened to make his actions known to Pharaoh. Moses had to run for his life, and it took him *forty years* to finally be on track with the timing that God had for his life. *Can you imagine that?* Read the account in the book of Genesis, chapters 2 & 3.

I must confess that I often struggle with the "Moses syndrome" in my daily walk with God. It feels like God is working too s-l-o-w in my situation. I am tempted to jump ahead of the window of time he has given me. I desire to see action now and not wait. I desire to preach my best sermon now. I desire to write my best piece now. The problem lies not in what I desire but in *losing sight of why I have the desires in the first place*.

I belong to God. I am His child. He is the Master and Lord of my life. It is His purposes that I live to fulfill, not mine. God is sovereign and eternal and is not limited by time. He is the Alpha and Omega, operating with all knowledge. My jumping ahead of God's timing does not help anyone, including me. When I do that I cause havoc not only in my life but also in the lives that God has placed in sync with mine, like my spouse and children. Solomon tells us "to every thing there is a season, and a time to every purpose under the heaven" (Ecclesiastes 3:1 KJV). Thank God that He is a God of second chances. That even when

I have messed up and "missed my timing" He resets me to the time that He has planned for me.

Word of Encouragement:
Trust God completely. Wait on Him. Speak to Him before you make a move and listen for His instructions. The peace you seek is in walking in God's timing. You may be wondering why there is so much turmoil in your life when you are doing all the right things. My question to you is: are you doing the right things in the wrong time? Like I do with my alarm clock, allow God to reset your timing.

Be blessed always.

_____
_____
_____
_____

My prayer today:

_____
_____
_____
_____

Singer Donnie McClurkin has a popular song called "Stand." The song centers on Paul's writings to the Ephesians saints.

> Wherefore take unto you the whole armour of God, that ye may be able to withstand in the evil day, and having done all, to stand. Stand therefore, having your loins girt about with truth, and having on the breastplate of righteousness;
> Ephesians 6:13–14 (KJV)

In the song, Donnie encourages the saints to "stand" after they have tried everything else and all options are gone. *Just Stand.*

Paul used a military illustration in advising us to stand. He shows the saints actively in combat, telling us how important it is to properly clad for the battle. One of the meanings of the word stand in the dictionary is "fight resolutely: to fight resolutely or give battle, often after having been in retreat." I need to make this announcement: We are in a war. I see the saints acting like we are on a vacation all the time. The devil is not taking a day off. He is actively waging war against us 24/7, 365 days a year. We must fight if we are to survive. We cannot just walk away. We cannot wish it away. We must stand, facing whatever situation is attacking us.

Word of Encouragement:
Stand. Cry if you must but hold fast while you are wiping those tears. Stand. Be resolved in your mind that you will win. God will not leave you alone on this battlefield. He is with you, fighting on your behalf. Face your fears. They will come down in the name of Jesus.

Be blessed always.

Today I am encouraged to:

_____
_____
_____
_____
_____

My prayer today:

_____
_____
_____
_____
_____

∞

Springtime is a beautiful season that I truly love. I like seeing the trees spring back to life and the beautiful array of flowers that spring up everywhere. *Wonderful.* I thank God that we have change of seasons.

I remember a few years ago, my family moved to Georgia after living for fourteen years in Miami, Florida. We had moved at the end of summer, and in my front yard were some plants—more like shrubs—that were green in color. By the time winter came around, these same plants were dead looking. Most of the leaves were gone, and the branches looked like dried-up sticks.

As spring approached, I surveyed my garden and decided that I would uproot all those dead shrubs and replace them with some bright flowers. I got my gardening tools ready to start the task and had the thought that I should probably wait, go the store first, and find the replacement plants. The next morning, as I watched my kids walk to the bus stop, something caught my eyes. In my front yard, where the shrubs were, I saw a beautiful bed of red flowers—tiny and plentiful. Who planted those? How did they get here? I ran outside to investigate and realized that the beautiful red flowers were the once dead shrubs that I was about to uproot. I later learned that they are called *azaleas.*

Sometimes we are too hasty to come to a conclusion, to write our children off, to declare our marriages over, to walk away from good friendships, to quit a job, or to switch churches. Just because a thing *appears* dead does not necessary mean it is. We may remain dormant while winter is going on in our lives; we often lose stuff, look dried up, and about ready to be discarded. Hold it! This is only for a season. Change will come. David reminds us in the scriptures: "Those that be planted in the house of the LORD shall flourish in the courts of our God" (Psalm 92:13 KJV).

Word of Encouragement:
Don't throw in the towel. God is not through with you yet. Just keep on living. I believe that God has great things in store for your life. Here is a little song that I want to share with you today.

> *Something beautiful,*
>
> *Something good,*
>
> *All my confusions He understood,*
>
> *All I had to offer him was brokenness and strive*
>
> *But He made something beautiful of my life.*
>
> *(adapted)*

Be blessed always.

_____
_____
_____
_____
_____

My prayer today:

_____
_____
_____
_____

∽∾

A few months ago God gave me this assignment to encourage others. He told me people were getting distressed to the point of giving up because of what they were seeing and hearing around them. It is trying times like these that cause us to make foolish decisions, because we allow our feelings to rule our thinking. I want to make it clear: I am not suggesting that I am perfect in this regard or that I am not in the same position as you; but as I encourage you, I encourage myself. I had adapted this statement that I use often and want to share with you. "Never make a permanent decision about a temporary situation."

Never make a permanent decision when you are hurt. One definition of the word *hurt* is "emotional or mental pain or suffering." Into every life a little rain must fall. It is part of what makes us human. "Man who is born of woman is of few days and full of trouble" (Job 14:1, NIV). People express their "hurting" differently. One person will secretly call all his friends, talk, and cry about it all night. Yet another will wear it like the latest designer handbag and show it to everyone who will look or listen. Some seek comfort in an addictive behavior, like drugs or sex. And I have seen others who did not shed a tear, did not tell anyone, had zero outward signs, and then they do a crazy thing—like hurt someone back—and we all get the telltale sign that inwardly they have been dying for a long time.

There is nothing to be embarrassed about if you are hurting. It does not demean you as a person. It does not mean that you are weak or dumb. It is not your fault, so stop replaying the events leading up to the hurt over and over in your head, telling yourself if only you had done this instead of that...It does not matter. You are human, and you cannot avoid being hurt.

If you believe you are partly to be blamed for where you are, then thank God for giving you the wisdom to see this. Confess to Him your shortcoming, accept His forgiveness and help, and move on. That is it. We learn from our mistakes. What the enemy wants us to do is to make foolish promises to ourselves that we will never be hurt again. Now you know that is a lie. You can still be hurt even if you did everything right. Just ask David.

He was fighting a giant, killing Israel's enemies, and making Saul look good as a king, and yet Saul sought to kill him until he had to run away from his homeland and those closest to him. But David did not go crazy and blame God and give up on his anointing. No. He knew his situation was temporary because God is true to His word (1 Kings 17 KJV).

Word of Encouragement:
Weeping is only a temporary situation in life. No one weeps forever. There is a season for everything, and, if you are hurting right now, I know it does not feel good. But before you give up on your child and write them out of your will or walk away from your marriage or separate yourself from God and fellowship, stop! Trust me, this too will pass. God heals the brokenhearted, and He wants to heal you.

Be blessed always.

_____
_____
_____
_____
_____

My prayer today:

_____
_____
_____
_____
_____

Previously I shared a statement, which has helped me. "Never make a permanent decision about a temporary situation." To recap: "Never make a permanent decision when you are hurt."

Today we will continue. Never make a permanent decision when you are angry. The prophet Nathan had come to visit King David, and he had an awful story to tell. He told him about two men in a city, one rich and the other poor. The rich man had a traveling guest, but instead of taking a lamb from his bountiful flock to feed his guest, he took the only lamb that the poor man had, killed it, and made a meal for his guest. When David heard the story, he was livid. "And David's anger was greatly kindled against the man; and he said to Nathan, As the LORD liveth, the man that hath done this thing shall surely die" (2 Samuel 12:5 KJV). Can you imagine David's horror when the prophet Nathan said to him "Thou art the man" (2 Samuel 12:7 KJV). He had just declared death on his own self. Read the entire account in 2 Samuel 12.

The dictionary gives the definition of *angry* as "feeling extremely annoyed, often about an insult or wrong; inflamed." It is one of those emotional traits that we are all susceptible to. I view anger like a volcano. It has a way of boiling underground for a while, and then it erupts and comes spewing out in its fury. And anything or anyone that gets in its way will suffer damage. You can be angry about anything or with anyone, even with God.

Many folks are angry with God. They blame him for the wrong done to them. Many of our children are angry with their parents or lack of them or just society as a whole. You see it as they explode in our schools and streets, and then the end result is death everywhere. Solomon tells us in scriptures: "He that is slow to anger is better than the mighty; and he that ruleth his spirit than he that taketh a city" (Proverb 16:32 KJV). The dangerous thing about anger is that you can be angry and not even realize that you are.

Word of Encouragement:
Anger is an emotion that has the potential to destroy you. Even though it cannot be avoided, it must be controlled, or it will lead into sin. There are many people sitting in prison right now who snapped during an angry escapade. And they made a decision that has permanently altered their lives. God has given you the power to overcome this. He has made you "more than conqueror" through Him. "Go ahead and be angry. You do well to be angry but don't use your anger as fuel for revenge. And don't stay angry. Don't go to bed angry. Don't give the devil that kind of foothold in your life" (Ephesians 4:26–27 MSG).

Be blessed always.

My prayer today:

_____
_____
_____
_____

※

We will continue from the adapted statement I have been sharing for the last two days, "Never make a permanent decision about a temporary situation." To recap:

1. Never make a permanent decision when you are hurt.
2. Never make a permanent decision when you are angry.

Today we will conclude. Never make a permanent decision when you are tired. We are all subjected to being weary—physically, emotionally, and yes, even spiritually. The prophet Isaiah tells us that "Even the youths shall faint and be weary, and the young men shall utterly fall" (Isaiah 40:30 KJV). Praying is absolutely necessary, but you cannot just sit and pray 24/7, 365 days a year.

Many of us find it difficult to say no to anything, especially causes we deemed as good or within God's will for our lives. I am so familiar with that trap. If you do not learn how to manage this, then you will burn out—a state where your body starts the process of shutting down until you give it the rest it needs. When you get to this position, you are operating without meaning. You are just doing, and I have to tell you, God is not getting any glory from you at this point. God requires us to have balance. Don't be fooled by those putting pressure on you to do more than God has equipped you to handle. One of the definitions of the word *tired* is "no longer interested; having lost patience or interest; overused." When our minds are in this state we are not capable of making sound decisions. We often say or do the very opposite of what we would have done otherwise. We need to step aside and get the rest our body, soul, and spirit need.

Word of Encouragement:
God taught by example, during the creation process, that rest is important. "And he rested on the seventh day from all his work which he hath made" (Genesis 2:2 KJV). Being tired is only a temporary state, but one that requires a right-now attention. Too many have shortened their life span and are having health problems because of this. Stop and listen. God may be using this time to refresh you, to hide you away until you are stronger. He loves you, and He cares about you.

Be blessed always.

My prayer today:

_____
_____
_____
_____

※

A new day means a new beginning. God gives us new opportunities to renew our thinking and refocus our attention on what *really* matters and not on the clutter that the enemy tries to put in our path. If you inhaled your first breath in a new year, you should have exhaled with a "thank you, Jesus" attached to it. *Hallelujah!* You've made it against all odds.

I must confess, I am not one for resolutions. This is not to say that I don't have goals, but I have learned that God's timing is always better than mine, and I rather do what He is doing in my life at this moment than to be pressured by false expectations. Be careful and don't allow the enemy to create an illusion about how to successfully attain your goals. Achieving anything requires work, work, and yes, *work*. If you are not willing to work, then you should not expect to accomplish anything.

Sitting around pouting and being jealous of others is just a waste of time and energy. Forget about blaming God for the color of the skies or being born on the wrong side of the tracks. Let me let you in on a little secret: When

God brings you to your promised land, the enemy will occupy it, and you will have to fight (work) to *rightfully* possess it. Why? Because what God has for you is great, and the enemy will always *try* to deter and frustrate you until you quit and forfeit your blessing.

The Bible gives the account of the exodus of the children of Israel from slavery in Egypt to a forty years ordeal in the wilderness. Finally they got to the Promised Land, Canaan, but the land had others *illegally* dwelling there. Their first obstacle was the people of Jericho, who refused to let them pass. Then they dealt with people at Ai, and then, as words of their success traveled, all the kings, "the Hittites, Amorites, Canaanites, Perizzites, Hivites, and the Jebusites; they came together to make war against Joshua and Israel" (Joshua 9:1–2 KJV). Talk about a group effort! People in unity to destroy you!

Word of Encouragement:
God has already given you the victory over every obstacle you will encounter this day. He wants you to trust Him and walk in faith. God's word to Joshua as they got ready to go across to the Promised Land is still for you today.

> I will give you every place where you set your foot, as I promised Moses. Your territory will extend from the desert to Lebanon, and from the great river, the Euphrates—all the Hittite country—to the Great Sea on the west. No one will be able to stand up against you all the days of your life. As I

was with Moses, so I will be with you; I will never leave you nor forsake you.

Joshua 1: 3–5 (KJV)

Be blessed always.

_____
_____
_____
_____
_____

My prayer today:

_____
_____
_____
_____

***

What was he thinking? He had been warned, and the woman had blatantly lied to him several times, yet he kept lying down and allowing her to seemingly, willingly trick him. Samson and Delilah. Read his account in Judges 16. The scripture says he loved her. *Aaaah, that explains it.* His being in love with her was against the very reason why he was born, because he was in love with the enemy he was sent to destroy. Sticky position. But before we start to judge Samson and point our righteous finger in his face, we may want to take a look at our own selves. There are issues in our lives that we are struggling with that we know will eventually destroy us, but we keep playing around with them because—let's be honest—we love it and the pleasure it brings.

John admonishes us to "Love not the world, neither the things that are in the world. For all that is in the world, the lust of the flesh, and the lust of the eyes, and the pride of life, is not of the Father, but is of the world" 1 John 2:15–1 (KJV). Sin has a way of sneaking up on us. We see it, yet we don't. Like putting on weight. We know we are eating more and exercising less, and yet when we gain weight we feign surprise and try to reason our way through it. That's what Samson did. He was told that if he shaved his head, he would lose his strength, but he had never tested it.

Maybe he thought that such a simple act would not really affect his ability, because what does the hair on his head have to do with his strength? Kind of sounds like what the serpent reasoned to Eve in the garden. "And he awoke out of his sleep, and said, I will go out as at other times before, and shake myself. And he wist not that the LORD was departed from him" (Judges 16:20 KJV). What a realization for Samson to finally understand that his disobedience to God had compromised his ministry and had rendered him powerless.

Word of Encouragement:

Pay attention to the warning signs that God places in your way to avoid the pitfalls of sin. Listen to the soft voice you hear within your heart, telling you you are about to slide down a slippery slope that will cause hurt and pain. After Samson was captured by the enemy, the first thing the enemy did was "put out his eyes" (blind him), and that's exactly what the devil is hoping to do to you. But God is faithful. In the end, He allowed Samson to regain his strength and still accomplish his purpose and to reach his destiny. And he will do the same for you.

Be blessed always.

_____
_____
_____
_____
_____

My prayer today:

_____
_____
_____
_____
_____

I started going to an exercise program a couple of days ago, and my instructor is an exercise "slave master." For about an hour nonstop she runs the routine, only giving mega second breaks for water as I try to keep up with the class. My first day was great. My body felt rejuvenated, and my mind was revived in taking such a positive step to improve myself. The second was good. I found out that the routine itself was more difficult with each day. By the third morning I could hardly get out of bed. My legs ached so badly, I was limping, and it took me forever to get down the stairs. Needless to say, I didn't feel so invigorated. I knew I didn't want to quit, so I repeated self-motivated phrases to myself like a mantra.

This reminds me of life in general. New things are normally exciting at first, but as soon as the reality of it sets in, the enthusiasm starts to wane. If we are not careful, we will never complete any task or fulfill any dream. Life is filled with starters. You will find folks starting their own business, writing the first chapter of a book, registering for their first class at college, and losing the first pound.

Life is also filled with quitters. Halfway through the big project, the first real obstacle comes—like getting a low grade on a test—and folks will walk away. Paul tells us in his writing that running in a race was not the main thing. It was getting to the end of the race that mattered. "Know ye not that they which run in a race run all, but one receiveth the prize? So run, that ye may obtain" (1 Corinthians 9:24 KJV).

Word of Encouragement:
Don't quit. You may be in pain right now, but keep on walking. It will get better after a while. Surround yourself with encouragers. Seek folks who have been down the way you are now traveling and listen to them. Read success stories about people who endured amidst their hurdles. Repeat a mantra if you must, but keep on going.

Be blessed always.

_____
_____
_____
_____
_____

My prayer today:

_____
_____
_____
_____
_____

∞

Personally, I do not know anyone who has endured suffering like the man Job as recorded in the scriptures. And to think he was a righteous man. His calamity was not a gradual process. All at once he lost all of his livestock—his source of finance; all ten of his children died, his wife walked out on him, and then his health failed. That's called stress overload. Yet Job maintained a right perspective. When it became too much for him to understand, he uttered the words, "God gives, God takes, God's name be ever blessed" (Job 1:21 MSG). I would love to say I am just like Job, that I uphold a correct viewpoint when trouble comes knocking my way. Honestly, I cannot say that I always do. But I find that I am learning as I mature in God to walk with a stronger faith, to shun the voices that speak in my head, telling me that God has abandoned me or some other negativity to let me lose sight of how much God loves me.

Trouble is common to all men. Saint, sinner, rich, or poor—"man that is born of a woman is of few days and full of trouble" (Job 14:1 KJV). I learned something when I worked with some dancers for a drama play I was directing. There was a dance routine that involved a lot of turns and spins, and I noticed that each time the dancer would practice she would still have her balance. She did not get wobbly or dizzy, the way the average person gets when one kept on spinning. When I asked her how she was able to do that, she told me before she starts the spin routine she must find a focal point—a stationary object or a stable place—that she concentrates on each time she makes the turn. She said as long as her eyes hit the focal point, her body's movement becomes secondary and does not cause any effect on her.

Job zeroed in on the focal point. It is not about the gift, it is always about the Giver. It is not wise to hold too tightly unto the gifts God allows us to have. Often we lose sight of what really matters and our frustrations and disappointments are because we have forgotten that it is not about us but is it all about Him.

Word of Encouragement:
God wants center stage of your life. Don't be overly concerned about trouble that comes your way. It happens to us all. Keep your eyes on God, and everything will be all right.

Be blessed always.

My prayer today:

Finally, my brethren, be strong in the LORD, and in the power of his might. Put on the whole armour of God, that ye may be able to stand against the wiles of the devil. For we wrestle not against flesh and blood, but against principalities, against powers, against the rulers of the darkness of this world, against spiritual wickedness in high places. Wherefore take unto you the whole armour of God, that ye may be able to withstand in the evil day, and having done all, to stand.

Ephesians 6:10–13 (KJV)

Make no mistake; the enemy does not want us to give praises to God

Praise God anyway.

Even if you don't feel like doing it, even if your circumstances does not dictate it.

Praise God anyway.

If you have plenty of money in the bank—Praise Him

And if you have not a dime in your name—Praise Him

If you are sick—Praise Him

And if you are healthy with no complaints—Praise Him

If you are jobless—Praise Him

And if you are secured in a good job—Praise Him

If you got food with your pantry overflowing—Praise Him

And if you are hungry and don't know where your next meal is coming from—Praise Him

If you have a roof over your head, your mortgage/rent is paid—Praise Him

And if you have no place to stay—still Praise Him

Word of Encouragement:
Meditate on the Word and Praise God no matter what. Remember you are a spiritual being living in a fleshly body. This battle is not yours it's the Lord's. God is present and will bring you out through all of your circumstances. So Praise Him through the good and the bad, for He alone is worthy to be praised.

Be blessed today.

_____
_____
_____
_____
_____

My prayer today:

_____
_____
_____
_____
_____

SECTION IV
DESPAIR & DEFEAT

> Be still, and that know that I am God.
> Psalm 46:10 (NIV)

Generally speaking, a lot of us do not think about God in the everyday simple things of life. We want to handle the "small" stuff, like buying groceries, and leave the big stuff, like cancer, for God to handle. But often an accumulation of "small" stuffs will, in a snap, bring disorder and confusion in our lives. For example, when there is no money to buy groceries, the stress begins to mount. You start warring with the government and the state of the economy, and then you move on to the church and their lack of social services, and eventually it gets to your household and those who loves you. Before you realize it, health problems arise. Getting in a fight about the things that we have no control over only depletes our energy and leaves us drained. When our backs are against the wall, it's time to stand still and look up.

It is good to know that God cares about all areas of our lives, no matter how big or small. In Him, we have a safe place where we can hide. No matter what is charging head on to destroy us, as frightening as it may get, we can be assured that "God is our refuge and strength, an ever present help in trouble" (Psalm 46:1, NIV). Think about it. The Bible gives an account of a young lad by the name of Daniel who was captured from his homeland during wartime by the Babylonians. Daniel was educated and skillful, and his gifting brought him to serve the king of Babylon.

But Daniel had enemies who hated him because "he had an excellent spirit" (Daniel 6:3 KJV), and before long he was dealing with an issue of having to decide between his worship to God and his service to the king. Note: enemies are a part of daily living. No matter how generous and loving you are, everyone will not like you or be happy for you. Daniel decided to follow God and, in the process, ended up being tossed in with a den of lions. God responded and sent angels to shut the mouths of the lions. "My God sent his angel, and he shut the mouths of the lions. They have not hurt me, because I was found innocent in his sight" (Daniel 6:22 KJV).

Word of Encouragement:
You are not able, by yourself, to bring about a change to your situation. You need the LORD. The only way you can get God's help is to be still. God will not move in your moment of confusion because He wants neither you nor the enemy to be mistaken as to the source of your deliverance. In the quietness of your spirit, listen to the LORD as He sends you help.

Be blessed always.

_____
_____
_____
_____
_____

My prayer today:

_____
_____
_____
_____

☙❧

One of the most compelling accounts of a woman who refused to be denied is the record of the Syrophenician women in Matthew 15. She was not a Jew by birth, and she knew that she had no "religious rights" to approach Jesus for help. But she had a devil-possessed daughter at home who was being tormented and probably causing much chaos. This woman's need drove her to seek help, and obviously she must have heard of Jesus and the many miracles He was doing amongst the Jews.

She sought Him out and made her request known. The dialogue she had with Jesus appeared *somewhat* hateful. On the one hand, there were the disciples, who detested her begging and wanted Jesus to send her away. Jesus said to her, "It isn't right to take food from the children and throw it to the dogs" (Matthew 15:26, NLT). Now at this point some of us would have lost our cool and most likely our blessing. But she did not get defensive. She replied, "But even dogs are permitted to eat crumbs that fall beneath their master's table" (Matthew 15:27, NLT). Jesus said, "Your faith is great;

your request is granted" (Matthew 15:28, NLT). And her daughter was instantly healed.

The enemy will always try placing stumbling blocks—obstacles—between our blessing and us. I have experienced this even at church services. There I am trying to reach God, and folks are looking at me all funny when I stand to worship. Some complain that I am too loud, too *whatever*, it doesn't take all of that, and I am only seeking attention. Others feel I am not righteous or "modest" enough. And the the list of criticisms even extend to include my culture, gender, age, educational status, and personality. Can you identify with me? I've even had folks tell me that my physical appearance does not fit the anointing I have on my life—that I can only go so far. The devil will use whoever will make him or herself available to him. Our prejudices can hinder the flow of God in our life, and worse yet, it can affect those around us.

Word of Encouragement:
Refuse to be denied. God will test your faith from time to time, and you may experience a temporary delay. But remember: delay is not denial. Keep pressing on. You will have to ignore the *haters* around you and keep focus on your goal. It is your need that will drive you to do the impossible.

Be blessed always.

_____
_____
_____
_____

My prayer today:

_____
_____
_____
_____

&

> Looking diligently lest any man fail of the grace of God; lest any root of bitterness springing up trouble you, and thereby many be defiled.
>
> Hebrews12:15 (kjv)

It is unlikely for one to get hurt and walk away without *some* damage. I've been there. You think everything is okay and then...*wham!* Out of nowhere, like a freight train, it comes bearing down on you, and if you are not careful, you will sink to a lower place than you had been before. As humans, however, we simply cannot live without the risk of getting hurt. Offenses are a part of living just as much as eating and sleeping. God is not worried about us getting hurt or even our hurting of others. It's how we choose to deal with it that is the issue.

As a part of my job, I frequently get calls from customers complaining about sewage coming up in the bathtub or basin. *Yuck!* When the problem is investigated, the root of a tree that has penetrated the sewer lines and caused a blockage is normally the culprit. To eliminate the problem, the removal of the tree is often necessary. But many customers are so attached to the tree that they have a difficult time accepting that it must be removed in order to bring a solution.

The LORD spoke to my heart this morning about this issue. He told me many are hurting and have allowed bitterness toward others, the system, and even God to take root in their lives. At some point they ex-communicated themselves, and, instead of exposing the problem, they watered it with malice, and it grew into large trees. Now they think they are tough and protected, and they walk around as if they are untouchable. Nothing seems to bother them. They carry on with an air of arrogance.

The real problem is not what is seen but what is happening under the surface that is causing trouble to God's people. The roots are blocking every good thing He has purposed for their lives. And they are dealing with *yuk*. The mess is coming up in unseemly places, like their children, their marriage, and their finances. God told me to prepare his people for the cutting down of trees in their lives. He is about to tear down every high place that we have built. He is bringing down every altar. Don't panic or be dismayed, because it is God's will for us to be healed. Many will feel exposed and vulnerable, but God is promising that His banner over us will be love.

Word of Encouragement:
Let the grace of God find you and bring you to a place of wholeness in Him.

Be blessed always.

_____
_____
_____
_____
_____

My prayer today:

_____
_____
_____
_____
_____

Be strong—When the storms of life are raging and your anchor is drifting.

Be strong—When the night is so dark that you cannot see your way.

Be strong—When you have more bills than money.

Be strong—When the temptation is great and your flesh is weak.

Be strong—When God is silent and your prayer is urgent.

Be strong—When you are lonely and the world seems unfriendly.

Be strong—When silently you cry and outwardly you smile.

Be strong—When God's will is not your desire.

Be strong—When you have no answers for the questions that are plaguing your mind.

Be strong—When it does not add up, and you feel like a fool.

Be strong—When you have done your best.

Finally, my brethren, be strong in the Lord, and in the power of his might.

Ephesians 6:10 (KJV)

Word of Encouragement:
God is a keeper. He promises to be with you always. I know you will make it. Be strong.

Be blessed always.

_____

_____

_____

My prayer today:

_____

_____

_____

_____

※

In everything give thanks: for this is the will of God in Christ Jesus concerning you.

1 Thessalonians 5:18 (KJV)

I've always had to do a double take whenever I read this passage of scripture. It doesn't just "jive" with me. In my mind I can easily think of so many bad experiences I have had that I am readily thankful about. I am certain I am not alone. Let me confess, the word *everything* is what I find to be a punch in the stomach. I know I am gasping for air when I think about it, because in my mind, giving thanks has to do with things I consider enjoyable—not the unpleasant, tear-dropping, heart-aching, life-is-so-unfair thing that I often have to deal with. So what exists is a conflict between what the Word of God says and what you really feel. Like a deer-caught-in-the-headlight moment. Most Christians just lie and pretend everything is just fine.

Since I know that God wants us to be honest in all our ways, and I know He does not need us to "sugarcoat" His words or analyze it to suit the situation, the question is: What does God expects of us? I know this is anything but simple, but here it goes. He wants us to trust Him. This is His will for us. He wants for us to have complete, childlike confidence in His plans for our lives. "Take my yoke upon you. Let me teach you, because I am humble and gentle at heart, and you will find rest for your souls" (Matthew 11:29, NLT).

Word of Encouragement:
Giving thanks is not an optional part of the Christian package. It is a commandment. So if you are walking right now in a valley of conflict and thanksgiving is so far from your heart that it can merely be uttered through your lips, give it anyway. Why? Because walking in obedience to God's word is more important than the way you feel. Don't worry, the pleasant days will be back, and maybe one day you will understand the total plan that God has for you. But never let your lack of understanding stand in the way of your thanksgiving.

Be blessed always.

_____

_____

_____

_____

My prayer today:

_____

_____

_____

_____

I believe most people have experienced a broken heart at some point or the other. It may have been your first "puppy love" that you had at thirteen. Oh, how you thought you would surely die, your world would fall apart, and your heart hurt so badly. Well…maybe not you, but I believe most youngsters have had that chapter. Don't we wish all broken heart issues were just as simple as a puppy love drama? But soon we learn that life can lead to complicated emotional ordeals, and your heart can be shattered in more pieces than you could have imagined. Recovery can become long and painful, and the damage often seems permanent.

The great news is, God heals the brokenhearted. Yes, He does. He will find every broken bit of your scattered heart and restore it anew. He is patient and kind and will not remind you that you may have contributed to the problem. No. God does not hold a grudge. He wants us to be healed completely. He wants us to be guilt free as He allows our confidence to be re-established. Jesus said:

> The Spirit of the LORD is upon me, because he hath anointed me to preach the gospel to the poor; he hath sent me to heal the brokenhearted, to preach deliverance to the captives, and recovering of sight to the blind, to set at liberty them that are bruised.
> Luke 4:18 (KJV)

Word of Encouragement:
No matter how badly you may feel today, God will heal you. God heals the brokenhearted. This chapter in your life is not the final one. Just keep on living; things will get better. Forgive yourself and move on. God will give you joy—unspeakable joy.

Be blessed always.

_____
_____
_____
_____

My prayer today:

_____
_____
_____
_____
_____

※

And the Lord said, Simon, Simon, behold, Satan hath desired to have you, that he may sift you as wheat: But I have prayed for thee, that thy faith fail not: and when thou art converted, strengthen thy brethren."

Luke 22:31–32 (KJV)

Praying is a practiced routine. If you fail to do it over any period of time, it will slowly but surely get away from you. If this happens, praying becomes difficult. You would be surprised how easy it is for your mind to go blank, and in two seconds you run out of things to say. Then it is an uphill battle to get your praying life to where you want it to be. It works like daily exercise. Knowing you need it and actually doing it is another thing. But if you start a good exercise routine and then stop, getting back in the swing of things can be tough at best.

I find it easier to pray for myself, not because I am a selfish person, but because I believe I am the most capable person to express issues about myself before God. Often too my needs are so pressing on my mind, it literary dominates my thought process, and there is little or no room for anyone else. Am I the only one? I don't think so. So when I go to pray, I am tempted to press in about my own issues—to cry out to God on my own behalf or those of my family. It takes real effort to genuinely pray for someone else—to stand in the gap for him or her, to cry when they cry, to feel the pain that he or she feels, to spend time in God's presence on his or her behalf. I have learned that often when people say they will pray for you, they are not speaking of spending quality time seeking God earnestly for your needs. Most times it is just a quick mention of your name in passing, like "LORD bless Ann today." While this may be appropriate, this is not the kind of praying I am referring to. In order to really pray for someone, you have to become a little involved in the person's life and his or her need. *Are you with me?* Jesus taught us this lesson when He prayed for Peter. He didn't just pray a blanket prayer for Peter. He was specific about what Satan wanted to do and what He had prayed about.

Word of Encouragement:
Praying for others will take the focus off your needs and help you to have a thankful heart before God. When was the last time you really prayed for someone? I normally write down the request, list the issues that I was aware of that need prayer, and read them before I start praying to make sure my mind is fresh. We are our brother's keeper, and we need to hold each other up in prayer. Take time today to pray for someone.

Be blessed always.

My prayer today:

I have walked this road before, I thought to myself as I looked around at the faces in the room. They were looking defeated as the drama production rehearsal was underway. Nothing was running smoothly. Folks were forgetting their lines, the dancers were just moving their bodies without conviction, the lighting crew was not coordinating properly, and the sound techs were not on cue. This was my first time working with the drama team at my new church, and I knew from experience that when a group of talented, creative folks got together on a project, the real challenge was in harmonizing the best from each person and channeling it into *one* presentation instead of a mirage of individual stardom. I looked with interest at each person's face because I also knew from experience that truly gifted people shine best under pressure. And *I knew* at that moment with all the confusion and deflated egos that we would have an excellent production.

That's one good thing about getting older—the wisdom you gain from experiences. I listen to my children's ranting as they make discoveries about life that I already know, and I smile inwardly. *Been there, done that!* So is it with our walk with God. "And not only so, but we glory in tribulations also: knowing that tribulation worketh patience; And patience, experience; and experience, hope" (Romans 5:3–4 KJV).

At first glance of Paul's writing to the saints in Rome, you would think he was insane to make such a statement. Why would anyone take glory in tribulation, difficulty, or distress? What good could ever be gained in being in such a state? A closer look at the writing, however, revealed the wisdom of it all. Tribulation sets off a series of events for hope to be realized. It has a domino effect: tribulation, patience, experience, and hope. I like the New Living Translation of this scripture:

> We can rejoice, too, when we run into problems and trials, for we know that they are good for us—they help us learn to endure. And endurance develops strength of character in us, and character strengthens our confident expectation of salvation.
> Romans 5:3–4 (NLT)

Word of Encouragement:
Do not run away from the problems that God allows to come into your lives. It has a purpose, and God has a plan. He wants you to develop and grow to be strong in Him. He wants you to enjoy life at the utmost, and you can only do so with tribulation, patience, experience, and hope. Smile at the next storm you see brewing in the distance. Enjoy what God has for you and let His grace, which is sufficient, carry you through.

Be blessed always.

_____
_____
_____
_____

My prayer today:

_____
_____
_____
_____

※

It's hard to appreciate light unless you are in the dark. The greater the darkness, the greater the appreciation for light, no matter how small it may be. Since I have relocated to Georgia, I have a newfound gratitude for light. In my new suburban town—which is quiet and dainty, almost rural—not all the streets are lit as in the city. I could travel for miles without any streetlights, and the night seems darker to me than when I lived in Miami. I have been lost a few times driving around town since I have relocated and have resolved that I will not travel at nighttime to any unfamiliar destination. Being lost at daytime is one thing, but at night my apprehension is heightened. Who knows what kind of evil lurks in the dark? "The LORD is my light and my salvation; Whom shall I fear?" (Psalm 27:1 KJV).

In life we will experience nighttime. A time when our vision is blurred and uncertainty like cobwebs spun all around our minds. *Nighttime* equals *dark time.* For many it is a time of confusion, anxiety, and yes, weeping. "Weeping may endure for a night, but joy cometh in the morning" (Psalm 30:5 KJV). David, I believe, had enough nighttime experiences to pen these words. He was the rejected son of his father, living and working like a servant in his father's house. His brothers did not regard him, even after God anointed him. He served faithfully for King Saul, even stood in battle for Israel when the giant Goliath threatened them, and yet this same Saul was hunting him like a wild animal, trying to kill him. David eventually had to find refuge in a strange land amongst him enemies. Yes, David knew about the night, but David knew also that daytime always follows nighttime.

Word of Encouragement:
I'm sure you too have had some nighttime in your life. You may even be having one right now. And it doesn't matter how bright the *sun* is outside, when your nighttime strikes it is pitch black on the inside. Only the *Son* light can penetrate the darkness on the inside and give you the correct perspective on the outside. Thank God that the *Son* light is not regulated by a solar system. You don't have to wait for a specific hour for Him to show up. Even now if you call Him, He will turn your nighttime into morning.

Be blessed always.

_____
_____
_____
_____

My prayer today:

_____
_____
_____
_____

Hold on, help is on the way!

Even a trained soldier will have times of weariness. If you fight long enough and hard enough, at some point you will get tired; you will need the help of others. Isaiah says, "they that wait upon the LORD, shall *renew* their strength" (Isaiah 40:31 KJV). The word *renew* means to replace something worn or to extend the time on something. Humans, with all our ego and vanity, are nothing but grass. Today we are fresh, and tomorrow we fade away. Ha! This puts it in perspective, doesn't it?

The urge to want to give up when you are weary is normal. I find that I am not as alert, my discernment is somewhat off, and my guard is down when I am tired. It is not the best time to sign a contract or make a commitment. This is when the enemy comes in for the kill.

Hold on, help is on the way!

God sends us help from unexpected places. He will not leave us without a way of escape. Just ask the children of Israel, as the Philistines in battle held them as captives. The Philistines had an advantage; they had a giant named Goliath. While Israel got weary from the enemies daily taunting, God sent help in the form of David, a young lad with no *apparent* battle experience. With stones and a sling, David conquered Goliath and then used Goliath's own sword to cut his head off.

Hold on! Help is on the way!

Word of Encouragement:
Do not discount the help that God sends you. Take the help God gives you and overcome your battles one at a time. When your help comes, do not allow pride to get in the way of your victory. It was this David that wrote: "He leads me beside still waters, He restores my soul" (Psalm 23:2–3 KJV). Are you weary? Don't give up. Hold on. Help is on the way!

Be blessed today.

_____
_____
_____
_____

My prayer today:

_____
_____
_____
_____
_____

∞

> Make a joyful noise unto the Lord, all ye lands.
> Psalm 100:1 (kjv)

When was the last time you really rejoiced in the Lord? How long has it been since you let go of your cares and just unconditionally praised God. You don't have to be a great singer or a talented musician to make a joyful noise to the Lord. What God desires is a joyful sound. I watched a talk show some time ago where an author who had studied the sounds that babies make claimed she understood what was communicated by each sound. I thought the show was somewhat fascinating, and, being a mother of three, some of the communicative sounds were familiar to me. Most can normally tell when a baby is unhappy—the piercing sound of a cry is not mistaken. Or when they are happy—the cooing sound of laughter is also known.

Is got me thinking. Can God identify the sounds we make? Does He know what we mean when words fail us and instead we just groan? I believe He can. God is listening for the sound—a joyful sound from the lips of His people. A sound that tells Him we believe in Him. A sound that says we trust Him. A sound that says we have confidence in Him and that we know He will bring us through. What sound is God hearing from us today? Is it a sound of doubt and fear?

Word of Encouragement:
Make a joyful noise unto the Lord. Give God the best you've got. Sing a song today. Forget about being in tune and all that. God is listening. What do you want Him to hear?

Be blessed always.

_____

_____

_____

_____

_____

My prayer today:

_____
_____
_____
_____

The odds are stacked up high. My confidence level is low. The probability of my getting out of this in one piece is a million to one. I have been battling with this issue for a very long time, and yet I am still struggling. I have the devil whispering in my ear, telling me it is time that I give up—telling me that God is not really listening and that my prayers are in vain. To be honest, I have so much self-pity right now that instead of rebuking the thoughts I am just cuddling and massaging them like a newborn baby whose life is dependent upon me.

Now maybe you cannot relate to what I am writing today because maybe, just maybe, you have never dealt with a "monkey on your back"—a weakness, a flaw, an imperfection that constantly nags you and makes you feel so undeserving of God's grace and goodness. I want to say to especially you, don't discount my testimony as useless. Keep this word hidden, because one day you will need it.

Now this brings me to the understanding about how human I am. And how powerful God is. As I sat in my pit of despair, I am bombarded with negativity. It is spewing out of me, and I hear myself indulging in the self-loathing words that are flowing unhindered, reminding me of the recent floodwaters I see in Florida, from all the rain. Then in the midst of it all, God spoke to me. A soft yet powerful word came to my heart, and, as I felt it prick me, I knew that the waters of my issue were subsiding. "What shall we then say to these things? If God be for us, who can be against us?" (Romans 8:31 KJV). One word from God quieted my storm. One word from God changed my perspective and my thinking. One word from God gave me renewed hope. I don't have to explain it, and I don't have to work out a mathematical equation to find the probability of this occurring. So I say, "Back up, devil. Let me be." What can I say? God is for me. It's plain and simple.

Word of Encouragement:
God wants you to understand that no matter what state you find yourself in, if you will even now turn your attention towards Him, He is faithful to bring to a place of victory and peace. Lift your head up and face this day knowing that you have divine favor, protection and strength from your heavenly father. "What shall we then say to these things? If God be for us, who can be against us?" (Romans 8:31 KJV).

Be blessed always.

_____
_____
_____
_____

My prayer today:

_____
_____
_____
_____

※

God always prepares us for the challenges we will face in our lives. *Always.* Before you fight your giant Goliath—and you will—He will prepare you on the backside of the desert by first giving you confidence in killing a lion and a bear. He'll give you a word today that seems so out of sync with what is currently happening in your life, and He will allow that word to germinate in your spirit, and then, six months later when the storms of life come blowing with a category five hurricane force winds, you find that you may sustain damages but you will not lose your life and your faith. That word will come rushing in like a barricade, and it will block every attempt of the enemy to destroy you.

Paul tells us in his writing to the saints in Corinth that

> There hath no temptation taken you but such as is common to man: but God is faithful, who will not suffer you to be tempted above that ye are able; but will with the temptation also make a way to escape, that ye may be able to bear it.
>
> 1 Corinthians 10:13 (KJV)

I wish I could tell you that once you become a follower of Jesus Christ life will become easier, and you would not have to deal with hard times, valleys experiences, dry seasons, and storms. This is not so. Many will testify that it seemed as if the heat intensified in their life and trouble came from everywhere once they became Christians. I know it because I have been there. But I have learned that God is faithful. You see, everyone has challenges, whether you are a Christian or not. Life is an equal opportunity player. How we handle the difficult times, however, is what separates us. Our reliance on God makes it possible for Him to lead us to "a way of escape," and our faith in Him guarantees our success as He prepares us to "bear it."

Word of Encouragement:
I am not sure what difficulties you are now facing, but I know you have them. We all do. Often you feel so unprepared to handle them, and you wonder why God even allows them to come your way. You cannot forget that you

are living in fallen state and are subjected to the events of life. God wants you to be prepared. He is even now actively working in your life, orchestrating the right people to be around you, sending a revelatory word for you because it is His will that you be a victor.

Be blessed always.

_____

_____

_____

_____

_____

My prayer today:

_____

_____

_____

_____

_____

It was a bold decision. It went against everything they had ever been told and what was customary. Tradition was a hard thing to defy, but they had no other choice. There was too much at stake. If they did nothing, they would lose everything. That's why they risked it all when they stood before Moses and the congregation and made their request.

> And they stood before Moses, and before Eleazar the priest, and before the princes and all the congregation, by the door of the tabernacle of the congregation, saying, Our father died in the wilderness...and had no sons. Why should the name of our father be done away from among his family, because he hath no son? Give unto us therefore a possession among the brethren of our father.
> Numbers 27:2–4 (KJV)

Change never occurs by wishful thinking. Change requires action. Stop talking about change if you are not willing to do something about it. Talk can be cheap, but true change comes with a price. I want you to understand that change is on God's agenda for your lives. It is *not* His intention that we be stuck, bored, and unfulfilled in the same place. God wants us to grow, to develop, and to increase, and all this happens with change. If a seed refuses to change, it will never germinate and grow into a plant. But the price is high, because that seed must be willing to be covered under ground and left alone. To be broken and die and then, from it, new life will spring forth.

Word of Encouragement:
Like the daughters of Zelophehad, you have to stand up and take the risk of rejection and even death to get to where you know God is sending you. Of course it is not

easy, but be assured that God is on your side. Today is your day for change. Seize the moment and walk out in faith.

> And the LORD spake unto Moses, saying, The daughters of Zelophehad speak right: thou shalt surely give them a possession of an inheritance among their father's brethren; and thou shalt cause the inheritance of their father to pass unto them.
> (Numbers 27:7)

Be blessed always.

_____

_____

_____

_____

_____

My prayer today:

_____

_____

_____

_____

_____

If you drive a car, you will encounter battery failure. I am sorry to tell you, but they do not just keep going and going as the commercial implies. They have a limited life span. Experience has taught me to always travel with jumper cables in the event that my battery life ends in an inopportune time. If this happens, I will need another car with a stronger battery life than my own, to *jump, recharge, restore* life, even though only temporary to get me moving. You get the picture!

If you are human, you will encounter failure, disappointment, frustration, discontentment, and dissatisfaction, just to name a few. Life will present challenges, and it is necessary for us to be prepared for it *before* it comes. Peter tells us to be mindful of this. He says to the saints: "Beloved, think it not strange concerning the fiery trial which is to try you, as though some strange thing happened unto you" (1 Peter 4:12 KJV).

Christians need each other to *encourage, strengthen,* and *support* them. I don't know about you, but I find that encouragers are a scare commodity in the body of Christ. Everyone is too occupied with his or her own sorrow to be of any help to anyone else. It is indeed sad. This selfishness has given a foothold to the enemy of our souls, and, instead of helping each other we often kill each other. We never know when our inopportune moment will come. When we are stranded by the wayside of life and just need someone to give us a little help to get us moving. Sometimes just being there with a hug or smile may be all that one needs to get him or her going.

Word of Encouragement:
Take time to extend kindness to someone. Not only does God expect it of us, but it will also help us in being a better person. I know life is tough and it is tempting to just pretend as if everything is all right, but when you are stuck you cannot afford to just sit there and die. Open up your "car hood." Get your "jumper cables" out of the car. Reach out to help.

Be blessed always.

_____
_____
_____
_____

My prayer today:

_____
_____
_____
_____
_____

This word is to all those who are in the trenches of life. You are in a battle, and it has been raging for a long time. You are crouching in these ditches, seeking protection from the fiery darts of the enemy. Of course you are weary and thirsty, and you are at the point of fainting. This fight is not only for yourself, but you are fighting for your children and your family. You have lived a mediocre life long enough. You have watched as your children have fallen prey to generational curses long enough. Poverty has been threatening you like an impending hurricane, and the vultures are circling, waiting for you to give up and die.

But God has a word for you.

You may not see it, but you are not fighting on your own. "The LORD hear thee in the day of trouble; the name of the God of Jacob defend thee" (Psalm 20:1 KJV).

You may not understand it yet, but you are coming out. "I waited patiently for the LORD; and he inclined unto me, and heard my cry. He brought me up also out of an horrible pit, out of the miry clay, and set my feet upon a rock, and established my goings" (Psalm 40:1–2 KJV).

You may not feel like speaking positively right now, but you have the power to make the right choice. "Death and life are in the power of the tongue: and they that love it shall eat the fruit thereof" (Proverb 18:21 KJV).

You may not look righteous, and some may even be judging if you are still a child of God, but you are whom God has declared you to be. And you are a recipient of His mercy and grace. "Shew thy marvellous lovingkindness, O thou that savest by thy right hand them which put their trust in thee from those that rise up against them. Keep me as the apple of the eye, hide me under the shadow of thy wings" (Psalm 17:7–8 KJV).

Word of Encouragement:
Trenches come and go, but the word of God will stand forever. In the short span you have on this side of life, troubles will come, battles will rage. Hold on. No one likes to eat dirt and wallow in mud, but I believe you are going to be victorious. If there were no wars, there would be no victories. Keep that in mind and start rehearsing your testimony, for it will be a powerful one. "Many are the afflictions of the righteous; but the LORD delivereth him out of them all" (Psalm 34:19 KJV).

Be blessed always.

My prayer today:

_____
_____
_____
_____

I love the TV sitcom *Law and Order*. I like sorting through the array of faces and identifying the "vic" (victim), the "perp" (perpetrator), and the motives behind the crime. I must confess that I could go hours just watching this show, and I am even guilty of watching the reruns. There is a certain degree of trauma associated with being a victim. There is emotional and often physical baggage, which is carried around every day. *Heavy load!*

It is not God's intention for any one of us to live as a victim. Even when life itself is the perpetrator, we should never live in that victimized mindset. The Bible gives an account of a woman named Naomi, as recorded in the book of Ruth. In short, Naomi, her husband, and their two sons relocated to Moab from her homeland, Bethlehem, during a time when the country was having a famine. In Moab, both her husband and sons died, and eventually Naomi moved back to her homeland. When she returned, her neighbors, upon recognizing her, started asking the question: "Isn't this Naomi?" Her response told exactly how she felt about herself. She replied, "Do not call me Naomi;

(my delight) call me Mara, (bitterness) for the LORD has dealt very bitterly with me. I went out full, and the LORD hath brought me home again empty: why then call ye me Naomi, seeing the LORD hath testified against me, and the Almighty hath afflicted me?" (Ruth 1:20- 21 KJV). Whew! Talk about a victim's mentality. This is the danger of living like a victim. You believe and live a lie, and you may never fully realize your true potential in God. Naomi thought God was against her because of her past and she would not have a bright future. If you read the whole account of Naomi, you will see that God gave her a fresh start, and she even had the joy of motherhood again through her daughter-in-law, Ruth.

Word of Encouragement:
God has great things in store for you. Don't let an event, a person, or a situation *perpetrate* you and allow you to lose sight of what God has for you. Hold your head up high. You are not a victim. You are more than a conqueror. "For I know the thoughts that I think toward you, saith the LORD, thoughts of peace, and not of evil, to give you an expected end" (Jeremiah 29:11 KJV).

Be blessed always.

_____

_____

_____

_____

My prayer today:

_____

_____

_____

_____

❦

> I have observed something else in this world of ours. The fastest runner doesn't always win the race, and the strongest warrior doesn't always win the battle. The wise are often poor, and the skillful are not necessarily wealthy. And those who are educated don't always lead successful lives. It is all decided by chance, by being at the right place at the right time.
> Ecclesiastes. 9:11 (NLT)

Do not quit. Whatever assignments you have started do not walk away from it.

This is not a sprint tournament, and it is more than just a marathon. This is a cross-country race of endurance where you are subjected to hills and valleys. Keep on running.

This is not a war of will power and human skill. This is spiritual warfare, where devils and demons are fighting for your soul, and you have to endure the hardness of the battle. Keep on fighting.

You must endure. You have the power to survive. You have the stamina to last.

Do not quit. Do not give up on your dreams. Do not doubt the words God has spoken to you.

Hold on to the integrity of your faith.

Be blessed always.

_____

_____

_____

_____

My prayer today:

_____

_____

_____

_____

※

I grew up on the teaching that you must work in order to get what you want. The frustration occurs, however, when you have done all you are supposed to do and you do not receive the results you are supposed to get. By all accounts, Peter was an experienced fisherman. He had a fleet of ships and was in business partnership with others. Yet after a night of hard work of fishing, Peter and others had caught nothing. Read the account in Luke chapter 5. Have you ever felt like this? I know I have. It feels like all your time and hard work was in vain. You took the high road and went to college, and now you can't even find a decent job. Does this mean your college education is useless? Are you bombarded with questions about some of the right choices you have made? What about living a Christian life? Is that also in vain? Of course not.

Many of us are like Simon Peter; we have cleaned our nets and called it quits for the day. We have settled into a position we are not comfortable with. We have lost the fire, drive, and fight within us. We are not actively seeking new options, avenues, or leads. We are no longer motivated, inspired, or enthused. Our smile is not real, our laughter is empty, and every day we wear disappointment like a cheap overcoat, trying to ward off the coldness of the situation we find ourselves in. Now I would love to tell you to just get up and keep trying, but I will be honest and say that most times it is easier said than done.

"And Simon answering said unto him, Master, we have toiled all the night, and have taken nothing: nevertheless at thy word I will let down the net" (Luke 5:5 KJV). I can imagine Peter's dilemma when Jesus told him to put his net back out to fish. His first thoughts must have been, *Why? What sense does that make?* In today's slang we would say, "been there, done that." I like the word *nevertheless*. It is the "undo" button on the computer of my life. It is my second chance to start over. It is my don't-feel-it, don't-like-it, don't-see-it, will-try-it-anyway release.

Word of Encouragement:
The Master of all creation is speaking to you. He knows every road you have traveled, He sees the hard work you have done, and He hears every cry you have made. He is telling you "launch out into the deep and let down your nets for a draught" (Luke 5:4 KJV). I pray today you will hear His voice and trust His words. Like Peter, your blessings will overflow to the point that you have to call others to help.

Be blessed always.

_____
_____
_____
_____

My prayer today:

_____
_____
_____
_____

Everyone has a story. An accumulation of experiences, hopes, dreams, and desires that tells who we really are. We all have had an embarrassing moment, a triumphant time, and skeleton we have hidden far away in the closets of our minds. It is my story. It is what makes me me. As unique as my fingerprint, my story is to me.

I am glad that God knows my story—*all of it*. And I am equally glad that His view about me does not change because of it. I would have been disqualified from His service if it did, because my story is not all filled with niceties. To say I have erred along the way is really an understatement. And I am not alone. "For all have sinned, and come short of the glory of God" (Romans 3:23 KJV). God loves us unconditionally regardless. He still beckons for us in the "cool of the day" and desires to have fellowship with us.

The apostle Paul, whose name was Saul before his conversion, is the author of thirteen letters in the New Testament. But Paul's story did not begin at this point of his life. Paul was a known enemy of the saints and took pleasure in seeing them persecuted and stoned to death. It was when Paul was going on one of these "persecution rallies" that he had a personal encounter with Jesus. "And he said, 'Who art thou, Lord? And the Lord said, I am Jesus whom thou persecutest: it is hard for thee to kick against the pricks'" (Acts 9:5 KJV). Even though Paul had such an undesirable past with the saints, he had perfect understanding of Jewish laws and zeal toward God. God used all these components of Paul's life and he became an effective witness to the saving of the Gentile nations.

Word of Encouragement:
God does not discount your story. He uses all your experiences. Even the ones you think are so embarrassing that you want to forget it. God can still use it. He uses your brokenness to help someone else. He uses your humility to reach a lost soul. He uses your shame to serve those in need and extend love and mercy to them. What is your story? Let God use your story to create wonders in the life of others.

Be blessed always.

_____
_____
_____
_____
_____

My prayer today:

_____
_____
_____
_____
_____

Dreams. Dreams. Dreams. The most literal meaning refers to the mental images that occur during sleep. Some folks dream every time they close their eyes. For the most part, my dreams are just a reflection of a tired mind, a busy day, an unresolved issue, or just nonsense. But sometimes they have profound—not just mental—images, and I awake knowing that God has just spoken to me.

We know from scriptures that God uses dreams as a means of communication. Joseph in scriptures is affectionately known as the *dreamer*, because his dreams were so ambitious that when he told them to his siblings it spurred rage, jealousy, and eventually cost him his freedom; he was sold into slavery. Read about it in Genesis 37. "And Joseph dreamed a dream and he told it to his brethren: and they hated him yet the more" (Genesis 37:5 KJV). The amazing thing about Joseph is that even in slavery he did not lose sight of his dreams. He knew that God had spoken to him, and even though his situation was trying to destroy his hope, his dreams held him in place. Like an anchor, God uses dreams to speak to us of our future and to prevent our faith from being shipwrecked.

I find that just as in Joseph's time, today dreamers are often treated with hostility. The more ambitious the dreams are and the more unwavering the dreamer is, folks just can't stand it. Even when humility is present it is still not a guarantee that those around you will not ostracize you. Yes, you may find yourself crying at times, wondering where you went wrong. Forget it. Do not even spend time thinking about it. *It is not about you.* It is about that which is already spoken about you. Remember the enemy comes to "steal, kill and destroy" (John 10:10 KJV).

Word of Encouragement:
Hold on to that which God as given you. Do not be too quick to share what God has given you with just anyone. Pray about it. Meditate on it. Then hold on to it as if your very life depended on it. It probably does. You may lose some friends, be often misunderstood, but don't stop dreaming and don't stop hoping. *Dreams. Dreams. Dreams.* These are your secret weapon from God.

Be blessed always.

_____
_____
_____
_____
_____

My prayer today:

_____
_____
_____
_____
_____

We have the tendency to behave as if whatever we are going through is exclusively unique to us, as if no one else has ever walked this road before. Of course this is not true because Solomon told us that there is "nothing new under the sun" (Ecclesiastes 1:9 KJV). Within the cycle of life, trouble touches everyone. We have all cried, been disappointed, and felt hurt, regardless of race or culture. The prophet Isaiah reminds us of our fallen condition. "The voice said, 'Cry.' And he said, 'What shall I cry? All flesh is grass, and all the goodliness thereof is as the flower of the field'" (Isaiah 40:6 KJV). That's it! We spring up but for a while and then we wither away.

We need to be mindful of our helpless state and turn our attention to the only One who is able to help us. For too long we have used God as a last resort. There was a song I used to sing in church years ago that says, "If you try everything and everything fails, try Jesus." Isn't that typical of us to only remember God after every failure? I can tell you right now that everything in this life will fail. If you are depending on the government to resolve the economic issues, then you are waiting in vain. Politicians are "grass"—just like you and me.

If we are putting our trust in a church leader, organization, or denomination to pull us out of our spiritual decay, then we are hoping in vain. Just look around you. Listen to the wind of the spirit as it brings the good tidings of our hope. I want to recommend Jesus. He is the void that you've been trying to fill for years in your life, and I know you have tried many things in search of fulfilling the emptiness inside. Let's be honest here. Our actions don't always show that we understand we need God. We wander sheepishly like spoiled children, determined to "do it my way," and only after we have hit rock bottom do we remember that we are but "grass," and we do not have what it takes to overcome life obstacles. Thank God that He is ever merciful and gracious to us. "In the day of my trouble I will call upon thee: for thou wilt answer me" (Psalm 86:7 KJV).

Word of Encouragement:
I know you have heard it before, but it still stands true: *Jesus is the only answer to life's questions.* He is patiently waiting for you to get out of your religious mode and dig in deeper for a relationship with Him. It's time to take your eyes off the imperfections of this world and focus your attention on the perfect, holy, righteous God, who loved you so much that He died in your stead. Don't be afraid. He wants to commune with you. "Come now, and let us reason together, saith the LORD: though your sins be as scarlet, they shall be as white as snow; though they be red like crimson, they shall be as wool" (Isaiah 1:18 KJV).

Be blessed always.

_____
_____
_____
_____

My prayer today:

_____
_____
_____
_____

※

The children of Israel had been slaves for over four hundred years in the land of Egypt. They cried to God about their situation and His promises made to Abraham, their father. God heard and sent a deliverer by the name of Moses. After ten plagues upon Pharaoh and the Egyptians, which ended with the death of their firstborn, the children of Israel were finally released from years of bondage.

Can you imagine the jubilation?
As Moses led them out of Egypt and they were maneuvering their exodus, they saw the Egyptians in hot pursuit

for their recapture. And wouldn't you know it, they were trapped with nowhere to run because they were surrounded by mountains, and the Red Sea was in front of them.

Don't be surprised if the thing—addictive habit, "besetting sin," low self-esteem, depressive monkey on your back, financial chaos, or the self-pity that won't let you let go of past hurts and failures that you have finally gotten freedom from—starts chasing you again. Yes, after you have fasted, prayed, joined the prayer line, got counseling, rebuked the devil, and claimed it and received it, you are finally free. And here you are two days, weeks, or months later, and you can feel the onset on the familiar feeling returning. LORD, *I need you.*

I love what Moses told the people.

> Fear ye not, stand still, and see the salvation of the LORD, which he will shew to you to day: for the Egyptians whom ye have seen to day, ye shall see them again no more for ever. The LORD shall fight for you, and ye shall hold your peace.
> Exodus 14:13–14 (KJV)

Hallelujah! Thank you, Jesus! You probably know the story. God parted the Red Sea and allowed the children of Israel to move forward. *Forward ever, backward never.* And while the enemy pursued, God destroyed them right before their eyes.

Word of Encouragement:
Hold your peace, and God will fight for you. The songwriter James Bignon sings "On the other side of through, there is a blessing waiting for you, hold fast, your troubles will not last." When Miriam (Moses's sister) got to the other side of the Red Sea, she got a timbrel and danced as she sang praises to God. Don't worry if you are going through a hard place right now; praise God anyway. Your blessing awaits you.

Be blessed always.

My prayer today:

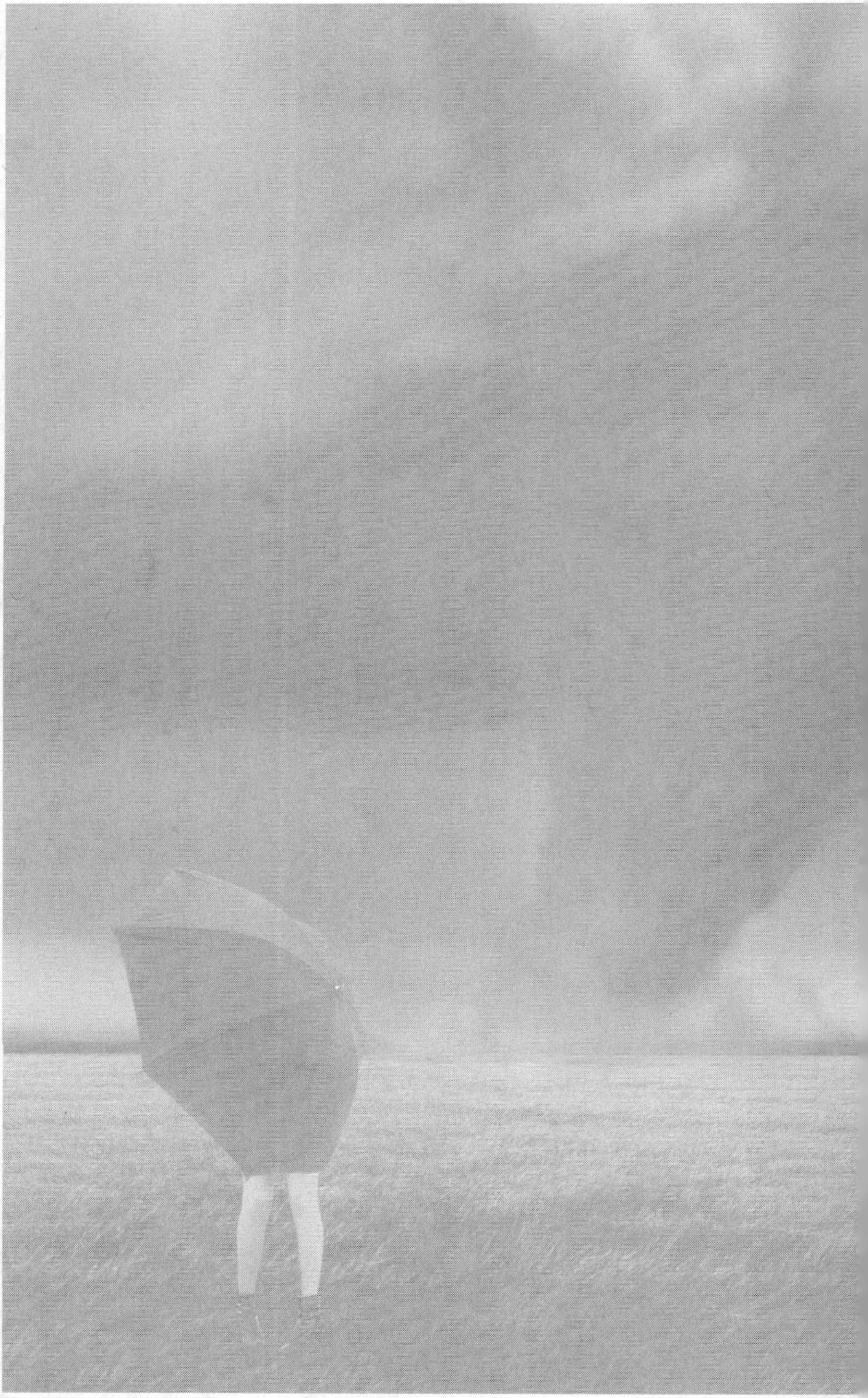

SECTION V
DOUBT & INSECURITY

God has not abandoned you. Regardless of how you are feeling right now, I declare that it is merely an illusion—a smoke screen—from the enemy to deter you from your rightful deliverance. God is with you. But don't just take my word for it; Jesus gave us His Word on it. "Are not five sparrows sold for two copper coins? And not one of them is forgotten before God. But the very hairs of your head are all numbered. Do not fear therefore; you are of more value than many sparrows" (Luke 12:6–7 KJV). Refreshing!

God is taking care of your needs. We tend to lose the right perspective about what our needs really are and why we are here. Then we whine and complain, and the enemy lets us think that God is not fulfilling His promises to us. Jesus tells us "Therefore I say to you, do not worry about your life, what you will eat; nor about the body, what you will put on. Life is more than food and the body is more than clothing" (Luke 12:22–23 KJV). Uplifting!

God is with you, for you, and eternally loves you. Unconditional love is not easy to understand. But God loves us in spite of all our shortcomings. Do not let the enemy trick you into believing that God no longer loves you because you have struggles. Cast down every lie of the enemy with the word of God. "Do not fear, little flock, for it is your Father's good pleasure to give you the kingdom" (Luke 12:32 KJV). Inspiring!

Word of Encouragement:
God has not abandoned you. He is taking care of all your needs, and He is with you and loves you always. Shake off the dust of doubt and walk with your head up high.

> Consider the lilies, how they grow: they neither toil nor spin; and yet Solomon in all his glory was not arrayed like one of these. If then God so clothes the grass, which today is in the field and tomorrow is thrown into the oven, how much more will He clothe you, O you of little faith?
>
> Luke 12: 28 (KJV)

Praises be to God!

Be blessed always.

_____
_____
_____
_____

My prayer today:

_____
_____
_____
_____

It's time to dream again.
It's time to reach for the impossible.
It's time to silence every critic and walk out by faith.
It's time to conqueror fear
Now is the day of salvation
Now is the time for renewals
Now is the time to hold on to what you have
For surely God has not brought this far just to leave you
He had not carried you this long just to let you fall
He had not saved you to let you be destroyed
You are able to endure hardship
You are an overcomer
You are special, loved, and lovely
You are God's child- He created you in His image
It's time to dream again.
It's time to rest and let God speak to you
Let Him ignite your mind and give you new ideas, insights, visions
Today He beckons you to not harden your heart.
You can, you will, you shall make it
It's time to dream again.
It's time to hope again.
It's time to believe again.

"For with God all things are possible"
(Matthew 19:26 KJV).

Be blessed always.

_____
_____
_____
_____

My prayer today:

_____
_____
_____
_____

Scripture gives the account of the first Gentile to be converted—Cornelius from Caesarea. He was a devout man who feared God, gave to others generously, and prayed always. One day he had a divine visitation and was told "thy prayers and thine alms are come up for a memorial before God" (Acts 10:4 KJV). Can you imagine that? Great lesson to be learned here! God sees and knows everything we do. Even if it seems like our efforts are in vain, don't worry. God is not mocked; what we sow we shall reap.

God used the Apostle Peter to be the "voice" to speak to Cornelius and his household and bring them the good news of salvation. But God had to first *convert* Peter's mind so that he could move away from his tradition to something new. Oh how our traditions can hinder the move of God in our lives. Even for me, God had to take me away from my comfort zones in order for me to experience a fresh wind of His anointing. I was so accustomed to seeing God operate one way that anything outside of the scope of what I was used to often made me hesitate.

I am fast learning, however, not to limit God by my tradition and to be flexible and open to *whatever* He does in my life. Peter's conclusion to Cornelius still rings true today. God is not a respecter of persons. *Profound. Revelatory.* "Then Peter replied, 'I see very clearly that God doesn't show partiality. In every nation he accepts those who fear him and do what is right'" (Acts 10:34–35, NLT). It does not matter who you are, God does not operate by our human standards. He regards you for who you are in Him, not what others think about you. He does not judge you by your past, and He is not worried about your future.

Word of Encouragement:
You can be all that God has called you to be. Some folks may not like you, and you may not even be given the respect you deserve. Keep on keeping on anyway. Do what is right. God is not a respecter of persons. Cornelius and his household received salvation that day. He became a first in his nation, the first Gentile to receive the gospel, and you too can become a first in your family and your community to do something miraculous.

Be blessed always.

_____
_____
_____
_____

My prayer today:

_____
_____
_____
_____

∞

Thank God that He does not have to consult with anyone—not even me—before blessing me! I am glad He does not have to get anyone's approval before granting me grace and mercy daily. He does this on His own merit, on His own virtue, and *not* on what I have or haven't done. His Word is clear about His intent to bless us. You ought to read Deuteronomy 28 and get a glimpse of the many blessings God has in store for you.

> And it shall come to pass, if thou shalt hearken diligently unto the voice of the LORD thy God, to

observe and to do all his commandments which I command thee this day, that the LORD thy God will set thee on high above all nations of the earth: And all these blessings shall come on thee, and overtake thee,

Deuteronomy 28:1–2 (KJV)

You don't have to be a scholar to know that a blessing is a good thing. Of all the bad things that come in our way daily, whether we are at fault or not, it is great news to know that God has good things for us. A lot of folks have a difficult time accepting the blessings of God. They are worried about the fact that they are not worthy before God. They question why God should bless them when they are not as righteous as they should be. Well, I have news for you. God already knows all of your imperfections. There is nothing hidden from God.

Word of Encouragement:
God is blessing you right now. Think about it. From the moment you opened your eyes today, many good things have come your way. You were able to move your limps, eat if you wanted to, drive to work, or just lie around and relax. Your blessings were waiting for you before you even opened your eyes to realize you would need them. *Awesome God.* It makes you want to shout and praise Him, doesn't it? Hope you enjoy the blessings you have today.

Be blessed always.

_____
_____
_____
_____

My prayer today:

_____
_____
_____
_____

I love the songs of the Psalms, and often I just put tune to them and sing them to the LORD. If you have never tried this, you should. You will be surprised how much melody God can give you, and I am a witness that your relationship with Him will go to another level.

I love to pray the Psalms. Some days, words are hard to express, and I find strength in just praying from the words of the Psalms. For those who struggle with prayer time and would love to pray for *more than a minute* without having a *repeat-a-thon*, then you will find this a great method to use to improve your prayer life.

I love to study the Psalms. I particularly study the lifestyle of David and get an understanding as to what event or circumstance may have inspired him at the time of writing. David was such an open and honest individual with his writing that he did not "sugarcoat" his feeling toward God. He asked questions of God, and many of his writings are prophetic.

I love to meditate the Psalms. Through them, I reflect on God's goodness, His loving kindness, His protection, His peace, His glory, His power, His majesty, His sovereignty, just to name a few. Within these songs are expressions that will strengthen you when weak, comfort you when sad, lift your head up when it's hanging down, inspire your creativity, and transform your worship.

Word of Encouragement:
Grab your Bible and find yourself a Psalm. The enemy has had you down for a long time, but today is a brand-new day. The possibilities are endless. Who knows what God has in store?

Praise ye the Lord.

Praise, O ye servants of the Lord,
praise the name of the Lord.

Blessed be the name of the Lord *from this time forth and for evermore.*

From the rising of the sun unto the going down of the same the Lord's *name is to be praised.*

The Lord *is high above all nations, and his glory above the heavens.*

*Who is like unto the LORD our
God, who dwelleth on high,*

*Who humbleth himself to behold the things
that are in heaven, and in the earth!*

*He raiseth up the poor out of the dust, and
lifteth the needy out of the dunghill;*

*That he may set him with princes, even
with the princes of his people.*

*He maketh the barren woman to keep house,
and to be a joyful mother of children.*

Praise ye the LORD.

Psalm 113 (KJV)

Be blessed always.

_____

_____

_____

_____

_____

My prayer today:

_____

_____

_____

_____

God is never in a hurry. Why? Because He is the Alpha and Omega, He knows the beginning from the end. And you cannot hurry God. He is not perturbed by the tantrums or the ultimatums that we make. We have to learn to wait. David says, "Wait on the LORD: be of good courage, and he shall strengthen thine heart: wait, I say, on the LORD" (Psalm 27:14 KJV).

I am not a fan of voice response system that is now available with most phone services. You almost never get a human voice anymore when you place a call. You have to plan not to be in a rush when you have an "urgent" task to accomplish, and you have to wait, wait, and wait. Then you may end up being transferred several times before you finally get to the person you need to speak to. Since my job involves dealing with customers on the phone, I try to exercise great patience when I am in these situations, because I know what it is like to be on the other end. I confess it is still easier said than done. I don't like waiting. It seems like a waste of my precious time.

Yet God wants me to wait. I feel like my whole world is crashing around me, and I want Him to act right away. I want Him to ride in like my knight in shinning armor and silence every devil. I want Him to speak loud and clear and tell demons to leave me alone, for I am His child. I want Him to hang a "don't touch this" sign on me that lets trouble run in the opposite direction; yet He whispers to me, "Wait." In the meantime my soul is crying, "LORD, how long?"

Word of Encouragement:
God has a purpose in all of this. He is not letting you wait to punish you. I know it feels that way, but never trust your feelings. Waiting does not mean doing nothing. It means that you acknowledge God's sovereignty over your life and you are willing to flow in his timing. God will always occupy you while you wait, because He wants you to be prepared for what is ahead.

Have a blessed day.

My prayer today:

I was learning new computer software in college, and I had a professor who was bent on teaching everything "the long way." My mind, however, is conditioned on learning through the shortcuts—completing the task by clicking on the software "icons." So I did *not* pay close attention during his lectures. I half listened to "the long way" method until he got to the shortcuts. Then it happened. I had a difficult computation for homework and the shortcuts could not help me. I had to know "the long way," which I had ignored during the lectures. You guessed it. I had to find the textbook and went fishing for information that we were already given.

Shortcuts. I love them. Give me a quicker, direct route any day. But I have found that God often works like my professor. He specialized in doing things "the long way." When He is preparing you for a task ahead, your destiny, or just your growth, He will not use a shortcut. If He is teaching you about faith, you will find yourself in a situation where your trust in Him is going to be challenged. David was anointed king of Israel when he was still a boy. Shortly after, he had his first "glory" moment where in battle for Israel he killed the giant Goliath equipped with only five stones and a sling. David found favor in the sight of the king and the people, and what looked like a shortcut to the kingdom took him seventeen years later to attain. In the interim, David had to be on the run because of a death threat from the reigning king, lost relationship with his best friend, had seventy-five priests dying on account of being associated with him, and finally he was alienated from his people and had to live with the enemies he would normally fight. Then God said he was finally ready! Read his account in 1 Samuel 17–22.

Word of Encouragement:
God will give you the best and only the best. If you are like me, you've had moments when you wanted to "name it and claim it" and hope that God would just give a "shortcut" to your blessing. You don't want to go through the process. You don't want to have to deal with "the long way." Take courage in knowing that God has your best interest at heart. You can trust His heart when you cannot trace His hands or see His plans. He knows what is ahead, and He knows just what you will need. "Those who know your name trust in you, for you, O LORD, do not abandon those who search for you" (Psalm 9:10, NLT).

Be blessed always.

_____
_____
_____
_____
_____

My prayer today:

_____
_____
_____
_____

※

I believe the first sign of bondage is when one loses his voice. If your voice—your "expressed opinion"—is taken away, you have lost your freedom. In a free society, your voice comes in the form of a vote. Just exercising that right by casting your ballot releases you from the bondage of whatever issues may be trying to limit you. Even if your vote is not the majority cast, you still experience freedom.

You can feel so guilt ridden that you surrender your "voice" especially when you are in the wrong. I remember my first fender bender. I was in the wrong, and I knew it. The driver of the car I had hit came out blasting. He did all the talking from the moment he got out of the car. It was a small accident. No visible damage to the car, but the whole ordeal cost my insurance $1400 and a hike in my rates. I learned that day that taking responsibility for my actions did not mean giving away my freedom. Even though I was wrong, it did not mean that I would lose my freedom to drive again.

Scripture tells us that the devil is the "accuser of our brothers, who accuses them before God day and night"

(Rev. 12:10 NIV). The enemy of your soul wants to shut you down, and he wants to take away your voice, your freedom. If you are like me when I am guilty or when I feel defeated, I get really quite. Internally I shut down as I wage the war in my mind about God and try to maneuver answers for the many questions flooding my mind. Why did this happen to me? Am I a failure to God? Is this a sign that God no longer wants to use me? What good can come out of this? Is this a generational curse? What did I do to deserve this? The Apostle Peter admonishes us in 1 Peter 5:8 (NLT). "Be careful! Watch out for attacks from the Devil, your great enemy. He prowls around like a roaring lion, looking for some victim to devour." God gives us an open invitation to find freedom in Him always. "Let us then approach the throne of grace with confidence, so that we may receive mercy and find grace to help us in our time of need" (Hebrews 4:16 NIV).

Word of Encouragement:
Speak up! Speak up! Speak up! Don't let the enemy intimidate you and tell you what you are doing is of no influence to the kingdom of God. Your voice matters. Your freedom matters. You matter. Even when you've made a mistake, don't just roll over and die. God still has the final say in your life.

The Apostle Paul tells us "Christ has set us free to live a free life. So take your stand! Never again let anyone put a harness of slavery on you" (Galatians 5:1 MSG).

Be blessed always.

_____
_____
_____
_____

My prayer today:

_____
_____
_____
_____

※

I love the way God speaks to us in the scriptures, especially the Old Testament. It displays human lives and nature in such practical ways that it allows me to understand that God still works with imperfect beings—like Adam, Abraham, Moses, David, just to name a few. These are men who, in spite of shortcomings, were still able to reach God.

Even with the issue of debt, the Old Testament is open about it. I have listened to many sermons that give the impression that accumulating debt is something new or "worldly" that real Christians never had, but Scripture tells us otherwise. Take the story of the wife of the sons of the prophets as recorded in 2 Kings 4. Her husband died and left her in so much debt that the creditors were threatening to take her sons into slavery as payment. Sounds familiar, doesn't it? This wife took action. She chose not to wallow in self-pity or to blame God for her situation. She went to Elisha, the leader of the prophets, and told him of her dilemma. She got the help she needed, and her debt was paid. "Then she came and told the man of God. And he said, "Go, sell the oil and pay your debt, and you and your sons can live on the rest" (2 Kings 4:7, NAS). Listen: taking no action is action itself. Not planning to succeed is planning to fail.

The apostle Paul admonishes us in his writing. He states:

> Be careful for nothing; but in everything by prayer and supplication with thanksgiving let your request be made known unto God. And the peace of God which passeth all understanding shall keep your hearts and minds through Christ Jesus.
>
> Philippians 4:6–7 (KJV).

Word of Encouragement:
There is nothing too hard for God to handle. Don't feel as if your hands are tied and there is nothing you can do. You can pray. You can voice your case to the omnipotent One, the powerful One. Even if words fail to come out of your mouth, your heart and mind can still speak. God cares about you, and if you just trust Him, He will bring you the help you need. God can get you out of debt. He

can provide you with strategies and open doors for you to have peace in the matter.

Be blessed always.

_____

_____

_____

_____

My prayer today:

_____

_____

_____

_____

Being lured into walking away from a good character is rampant amongst us. At the visible head of the lists are our leaders, but that does not mean they are the only guilty ones. We are all susceptible to faulty human traits that in a moment pull us under to a place from where it is hard to recover. Gehazi's story, as recorded in 2 Kings 5, is a prime example of how one can allow greed and envy to entrap them into a place of destruction. Gehazi worked as servant to the Prophet Elisha, who was famous for working miracles in Israel.

Naaman, the captain of the Syrian army, had leprosy and had come to Elisha for his help in receiving healing. As was customary, Naaman bought with him gold and fine clothing as an offering to Elisha, who refused the offering but helped Naaman to obtain his healing. But Gehazi's lust was ignited, and he told Naaman a lie about Elisha changing his mind and taking the stuff. His greed became a curse to him and his seed forever because he was inflicted with the same leprosy from which Naaman was healed. "Naaman's leprosy will cling to you and to your descendants forever. Then Gehazi went from Elisha's presence and he was leprous, as white as snow" (2 Kings 5:27, NIV).

Gahazi failed the character test. The dictionary gives the meaning of *character* as "distinctive qualities: the set of qualities that make somebody or something distinctive." We have to be careful that we too do not fail God's character test. And yes, God is going to give us a character test. He is more interested in our character than our gifting, money, and talent. What you do when you're in the saints' presence is just as important as when you are not. There are daily opportunities for us to be tested and for us to fail, like taking the extra change we get at the checkout counter and calling it a blessing, lying to our creditors that the check is in the mail, stealing the parking spot you saw a car waiting on, or writing a "rubber" check in church just to impress those sitting beside you.

Daily, God gives us character tests. People gifting and anointing does not awe me anymore. I want to know if you have character. I want to know what kind of husband/wife/parent/child/employee/employer you are. Like Gehazi, some of the things we do today are laying traps for our generations to follow. Jesus told us,

> "Let your light so shine before men, that they may see your good works, and glorify your Father which is in heaven"
>
> (Matthew 5:16 KJV)

Word of Encouragement:
Determine within yourself to be a person of character. It will never fail you. You are the only Bible that many people see, and God is depending on you to be a true witnesses. Does that mean you are perfect? Oh no. But you should strive for perfection and maturity. There is a church hype over anointed folks. I pray the hype would be about a child of character. God is giving you a character test today? Are you prepared?

Be blessed always.

_____
_____
_____
_____

My prayer today:

_____
_____
_____
_____

※

God is a healer. The meaning of the word heal is "to restore a person, body part, or injury to health." I have read, heard, and witnessed people being physically healed. My own mother was healed of cancer years ago and still has the doctors speechless about what her test had shown and finding nothing after they went in to remove the cells. There is no question in my mind that God still heals the physical body, and when I am sick I pray for healing, expecting Him to work on my behalf.

A deeper meaning of the word heal, however, is "to recover spiritually or emotionally: to get rid of a wrong, evil, or painful affliction." When Jesus healed someone while he was on earth, he often used the phrase "be made whole." He heals them physically, but then he would go further and declared that person whole.

The gospel according to St. Luke gives an account of a woman who experienced total healing from Jesus. "And a woman who had a hemorrhage for twelve years and could not be healed by anyone" (Luke 8:43, NAS). She had tried the doctors without avail and had lost all her money in medical expenses. Eventually, she had a dramatic encounter with Jesus that stopped the bleeding and healed her physically. But in addition, she was healed emotionally and spiritually. "And he said unto her, Daughter, be of good comfort, thy faith hath made thee whole; go in peace" (Luke 8:48 KJV).

Wow! God wants to heal more than just your physical body. He wants you to have complete healing in your soul. Many of us look good on the outside, but inwardly our spirit is so broken. We know how to wear nice clothes to cover up any physical blemishes we may have, but there is nothing we can buy to cover up a broken soul. When our soul is broken and in need of healing, it comes out in some awkward ways and places—like suppressed anger that explodes like a volcano and destroys anything in its path, like a drug addict or an alcoholic who keeps going back to the same place of misery. Like an inmate walking back and forth through the revolving doors of the prison system. God is a healer.

Word of Encouragement:
Seek healing for the hidden areas of your life. Don't be so focused with your physical self and totally ignore your spirit and soul. Society has made accommodations for many physical challenges. We have handicapped parking and special education classes. These are the obvious things we can see. God wants you to bring to Him the not-so-obvious things. The things that are really eating away at your peace and destroying your walk with Him.

Be blessed always.

_____

_____

_____

_____

My prayer today:

_____

_____

_____

_____

◈

Sarah is listed as one of the patrons of faith in the book of Hebrews. She was the wife of Abraham, barren, and was promised a child by God. After waiting and not seeing the fulfillment of this promise, Sarah decided to give Abraham a child by means of a surrogate mother, her handmaid. Maybe she thought she would help God out. It may have been common knowledge about God's promises to Abraham, and, who knows, she may have felt it was her fault—since she could not conceive—why his blessings were not fulfilled. Who knows? Maybe low self-esteem had started to settle in.

Twenty-five years later Sarah learned that "God is not slack concerning his promises" (2 Peter 3:9 KJV). If He said it, then that settles it. By this time Sarah was now too old, and childbearing was out of the equation. But don't you love it that God's promises are not hindered by anything? "For with God nothing shall be impossible" (Luke 1:37 KJV). When Sarah heard that she was still going to have a child at the age of ninety-nine, she laughed. Maybe it was a nervous laugh, like the one you give when something seems too good to be true. I am encouraged by the faith of Sarah. Hebrews 11:11(KJV) states, "Through faith also Sara herself received strength to conceive seed, and was delivered of a child when she was past age, because she judged him faithful who had promised."

Word of Encouragement:
Maybe you have been waiting a long time for a fulfillment of a promise, and it seems like it is not coming through. In the interim you may have tried to help God out with some temporary fixes on your own. Like Sarah, you will find out that God does not need your help with any promise He has given you. And that disobedience to God's Word has serious consequences. Hold it. God is faithful. God is true. God is not through with you yet. Praise Him today and thank Him in advance for fulfilling every promise He has given you. "And blessed is she that believed: for there shall be a performance of those things which were told her from the LORD" (Luke 1:45 KJV).

Be blessed always.

_____
_____
_____
_____

My prayer today:

_____
_____
_____
_____

※

Picture this scene. Two brothers were in a business partnership. One day they were busy working when a stranger walk by and stop to talk. The stranger asked them to leave their present business and come with him, as he had a better proposal. The two brothers immediately went with the stranger. Ludicrous, isn't it? This story is the true record of the starting of Peter and Andrew's ministry with Jesus in Matthew 4:18–19 (KJV):

> And Jesus, walking by the sea of Galilee, saw two brethren, Simon called Peter, and Andrew his

brother, casting a net into the sea: for they were fishers. And he saith unto them, Follow me, and I will make you fishers of men. And they straightway left their nets, and followed him.

Oftentimes the call of God on one's life does not seem to be rationale. No it is not crazy-stupid, but looking with the naked eye, it may not be a levelheaded, sensible thing to be doing. Often there is no reference. You may be the first person in your family or environment that God chooses to use that way. Like when God called Abraham to go to a country that he had never seen. How could Abraham explain that to his family? Or Mary who was called to bear a child even though she was a virgin and would risk being stoned to death for her actions. What do you say to your friends?

Having a faith walk with God is neither undemanding nor trivial. I can share from my own experiences that it requires courage, trust, tenacity, humility, and the willingness to sometimes look ridiculous in the face of your peers. Forget trying to explain yourself to everyone or getting them to see what you see. God will orchestrate the right people to come into your life to encourage, support, and pray for you.

Word of Encouragement:
Your better days are ahead of you. What God has in store for you is great. He is still walking by and calling "follow me." As you leave your safety "nets," He promises that He will transform you to become "fishers of men," so that you

will be able to reach all mankind with the wonder of His love.

Be blessed always

_____
_____
_____
_____
_____

My prayer today:

_____
_____
_____
_____

The Bible gives an account of a man who was sick of the palsy. He was paralytic and was confined to the bed. Four friends took him to a house that Jesus was teaching at so that he could get his healing. Thank God for friends. When they got there the place was crowed, so much so that they were unable to even get to the door. But these friends were not to be deterred. They took him up to the roof of the house, took the roof off, and lowered him to see Jesus. "And, behold, they brought to him a man sick of the palsy, lying on a bed: and Jesus seeing their faith said unto the sick of the palsy; Son, be of good cheer; thy sins be forgiven thee" (Matthew 9:2 KJV). It was the faith of the friends that Jesus commented on, and it was their faith that brought healing to the sick man.

I want to thank God for friends. What would we do without them? Friends who stands by us during the good times and the bad. Honest friends who will not let us off the hook for being ugly to others but will love us anyway. Friends who understand us enough that we don't have to say everything. Friends who encourages us when we're down and tell us not to quit. Friends who will pray, cry, and rejoice with us. Thank God for friends.

Word of Encouragement:
Reach out today to all your friends. God loves you enough to have blessed you with them. Don't take them for granted, for they are precious. The Word of God tells us "a man that hath friends must shew himself friendly" (Proverbs 18:24 KJV).

Be blessed always.

_____
_____
_____
_____

My prayer today:

_____

_____

_____

_____

***

As believers in Christ, we need to be consistent in what we do, say, and be. We should operate from a higher spiritual, physical, and moral standard. Our leaders are not politicians who have to entice us with sweet words in order to retain our membership, loyalty, and money. The church is not a social club where people are accepted or rejected according to their bank accounts, which side of the tracks they live on, or how they look. Promotion in the church is not governed by whom we know, whose shoulders we rub, or from which families we are born.

Understanding who we are is in direct correlation to the way we act. People who think defeated never act victorious. Even if they try, the attempt is normally superficial and so bogus, and they do not possess the strength to carry it out for a long period of time. In other words, eventually, however you think will come out in the way you act. "For as a man thinks in his heart so is he" (Proverbs 23:7, NKJV). The best mirror to look in to find out who we are is the Bible, the Word of God. Only what God says about us is true. All other sources—family, friends, enemies—are distorted and tainted and will not give you a clear, true picture.

So who are we? The apostle Peter tells us "But ye are a chosen generation, a royal priesthood, an holy nation, a peculiar people; that ye should shew forth the praises of him who hath called you out of darkness into his marvellous light" (1 Peter 2:9 KJV). Awesome! It is from this platform that our thinking must be shaped. Once we embrace this and walk according to what God calls us, then we will have little difficulty displaying to the world what being a child of God is all about. It is time for us to stop living below who we are called to be. Now is the time to shine forth His light in the darkness of the world. The world is looking to us, more so in these hard times, for Christians who are reliable, dependable, and who will live what they profess.

Word of Encouragement:
You are a Christian—follower of Christ. Your goal is to walk, talk, and live in perfect harmony to the teachings and principles of Christ. Be mindful that for many, you are the only "Bible" they will read. Think about it. As they turn the pages of your lives, let your testimony be one that is pleasing to God.

Be blessed always.

_____
_____
_____
_____

My prayer today:

_____
_____
_____
_____

∞

> I beseech you therefore, brethren, by the mercies of God, to present your bodies a living sacrifice, holy, acceptable to God, which is your spiritual service.
> Romans 12:1 (ASV)

The dictionary gives the meaning of sacrifice as "giving up of something valued: a giving up of something valuable or important for somebody or something else considered to be of more value or importance." I discovered the harsh truth about sacrifices one day in prayer while I was soliciting God's attention, stating the many sacrifices that I had presumably made for the "gospel's sake." The Lord told me He was not concerned about what I had given up but rather why I had given it up. Plainly stated, the Lord said, "If it does not mean anything to you, it does not mean anything to God." Whew! He really had my attention!

God is not looking for martyrs. You really don't need to prove a point to God about how good you are or how willing you are to stand you for Him. The Bible gives the account of God calling Abraham to sacrifice Isaac, his promised son. Abraham had already lost his first son, Ishmael, when he had to send him away with his mother, Hagar. It had taken Abraham twenty-five years of waiting on God for this promised son, and now to be told to sacrifice him to the Lord was a hard thing. But Abraham obeyed God. His heart was in the right place, and even though God did not allow him to kill the boy, God knew that obeying Him was worth more to Abraham than even the promised son. Read the account in Genesis 22.

As the Lord continued to minister to me I realized that some things are not a sacrifice unless I understand the value of it. For years, when I struggled with low self-esteem the idea of giving up of me to God was really not a sacrifice at all. Why? Because I did not place value in myself. In essence, even though I would give up of my time in working in church events, it was not a real sacrifice because it really meant nothing to me—it was easy for me to do. Now I walk in the understanding of what a real sacrifice is, and I have allowed the Lord to help me find myself in Him.

Word of Encouragement:
God wants all of you. He is willing and able to work with you so that you can present your body to Him as a living sacrifice. Pray today that He opens your eyes to the sacrifices that He is requiring of you.

Be blessed always

_____
_____
_____
_____

My prayer today:

_____
_____
_____
_____

※

She woke up early, got some water, and took a bath. She wanted to get rid of any odor from the night before, but mainly she needed to calm her nerves. Today was the day. It's been such a long journey, and she was so weak but she had to do this. She had to feel alive again. She got dressed and covered her head with her shawl. She was not taking any chances of being caught, because it would have serious consequences.

She heard the noise long before she saw Him. Some guy—rich by the telling of his clothes—had His attention. As she watched she saw Him walking away. Fear gripped her like chains shackled to her ankles, and she could not move. It had to be now or never. She knew she would never have this opportunity twice. She ran, joining up with the crowd, and, as she stretched out her hands to stop Him, she fell, her hands touching the edge of his clothes.

She felt it instantly. A surge of energy had erupted within her body—a miracle. She felt the dark clouds shifting and a bright light occupying her space. In Isaiah's prophesy about Christ in chapter 61:3, he wrote

> To appoint unto them that mourn in Zion, to give unto them beauty for ashes, the oil of joy for mourning, the garment of praise for the spirit of heaviness; that they might be called trees of righteousness, the planting of the LORD, that he might be glorified.

This is what she felt—an exchange. God took away all the mess of her life and replaced it with His blessings.

The dramatization depicts the story of the "woman with the issue of blood" as told in the Gospel of Luke, chapter 8. What about you today? Is there something you need from God that seems farfetched? Has fear suffocated your faith and left you afraid to move? Maybe you have been ostracized by others, and you are so ashamed of your past mistakes and failures.

Word of Encouragement:
The voice of the LORD speaks to you, and he wants to give you an extraordinary exchange. He wants you to let go of all the ugliness in your life and receive the beauty of His spirit. Come on. Take a step toward your freedom. What awaits you will change your life.

Be blessed always.

_____
_____
_____
_____
_____

My prayer today:

_____
_____
_____
_____
_____

Have you ever wondered if God is truly hearing and listening to you? I know I have had my moments when prayers seemed unanswered, and my faith begins to waver, and I am tempted to believe that talking to God is a waste of time.

I love the answer that the apostle John writes to the church at a time when he may have had similar questions like mine. He writes:

> And this is the confidence that we have in him, that, if we ask any thing according to his will, he heareth us: And if we know that he hear us, whatsoever we ask, we know that we have the petitions that we desired of him.
>
> 1 John 5:14–15 (KJV)

Did you read that? I hope you did not miss it. We can have confidence that God is listening to us. He hears us.

According to the dictionary, one of the definitions for the word confidence is a "trusting relationship: a relationship based on trust and intimacy." Having a relationship with God based on His faithfulness and our trust is the very foundation of our existence. This is why the enemy of our souls tries so hard to steal, kill, or destroy it. But don't you let him!

Word of Encouragement:
God loves you. He hears you, and He is even now working on your behalf. I have found that He not only hears the words that proceed out of our mouths but also hears the words (thoughts) that we are sometimes too afraid to utter. Right now you have the opportunity to make a petition to the King of kings. What will your request be? What is your desire of Him?

Be blessed always.

_____
_____
_____
_____
_____

My prayer today:

_____
_____
_____
_____
_____

> And Peter answered him and said, Lord, if it be thou, bid me come unto thee on the water. And he said, Come. And when Peter was come down out of the ship, he walked on the water, to go to Jesus.
>
> Matthew 14:28–29 (KJV)

Permission granted.

No one had ever walked on water before. No one has ever walked on water since. Swimming is not an everyday activity for most people. Many fear the insecure feeling that water gives: no solid place to put their feet. We love security and being able to stand sure-footed on whatever we are doing. No one I have ever met enjoys God stretching him or her; it can be really scary. But He knows that unless He orchestrates situations that grant us an opportunity to exercise our faith, we would never mature in Him.

Jesus beckons us to the impossible...all of us, not just a chosen few. It was not only Peter who was sitting in the ship in the midst of a boisterous sea that night when Jesus came walking toward them on the water. The sight must have been spectacular. But, like all of us—when God does something outside of our human normalcy, we become afraid.

Fear is paralyzing. Faith is liberating.

When Jesus said "come" in response to Peter's request, all twelve disciples had the same opportunity to act. Only one man—Peter—stood up, put his feet outside of the safety of the ship, and walked. Only one man—Peter—understood: Permission granted.

Word of Encouragement:
If God is calling you to start that business, write that book, go into ministry, get married, start a new career, return to the classroom, whatever He is saying to you: Permission granted. Don't be intimated by those around you who chose to sit in the safety of the ship and try to sway you as to the impossibility of your situation. Sure you don't have enough money, time, or resources. And you may have been born on the wrong side of the tracks, have generational issues, and overlooked by those around you. Jesus still says: Permission granted.

Walk out on the impossible, for God has empowered you to succeed.

Be blessed always

_____
_____
_____
_____
_____

My prayer today:
___
___
___
___

TO CONTACT AUTHOR:

http://charmaingriffiths.tateauthor.com
http://charmaingriffiths.blogspot.com
http://thebookmarketingnetwork.com